# Computer Vision in the Infrared Spectrum

## Challenges and Approaches

t

# Synthesis Lectures on Computer Vision

Editors
**Gérard Medioni,** *University of Southern California*
**Sven Dickinson,** *Samsung Toronto AI Research and University of Toronto*

Synthesis Lectures on Computer Vision is edited by Gérard Medioni of the University of Southern California and Sven Dickinson of the University of Toronto. The series publishes 50- to 150 page publications on topics pertaining to computer vision and pattern recognition. The scope follows the purview of premier computer science conferences, and includes the science of scene reconstruction, event detection, video tracking, object recognition, 3D pose estimation, learning, indexing, motion estimation, and image restoration. As a scientific discipline, computer vision is concerned with the theory behind artificial systems that extract information from images. The image data can take many forms, such as video sequences, views from multiple cameras, or multi-dimensional data from a medical scanner. As a technological discipline, computer vision seeks to apply its theories and models for the construction of computer vision systems, such as those in self-driving cars/navigation systems, medical image analysis, and industrial robots.

Image-Based Modeling of Plants and Trees
Sing Bing Kang and Long Quan
2009

Computer Vision in the Infrared Spectrum: Challenges and Approaches

Michael Teutsch, Angel D. Sappa, and Riad I. Hammoud

ISBN: 978-3-031-00698-2    paperback
ISBN: 978-3-031-01826-8    PDF
ISBN: 978-3-031-00083-6    hardcover

DOI 10.1007/978-3-031-01826-8

A Publication in the Springer series
*SYNTHESIS LECTURES ON COMPUTER VISION*

Lecture #19
Series Editors: Gérard Medioni, *University of Southern California*
                Sven Dickinson, *Samsung Toronto AI Research and University of Toronto*
Series ISSN
Print 2153-1056    Electronic 2153-1064

# Computer Vision in the Infrared Spectrum

## Challenges and Approaches

Michael Teutsch
Hensoldt Optronics, Germany

Angel D. Sappa
ESPOL Polytechnic University, Ecuador
Computer Vision Center (CVC), Spain

Riad I. Hammoud
TuSimple, USA

*SYNTHESIS LECTURES ON COMPUTER VISION #19*

# ABSTRACT

Human visual perception is limited to the visual-optical spectrum. Machine vision is not. Cameras sensitive to the different infrared spectra can enhance the abilities of autonomous systems and visually perceive the environment in a holistic way. Relevant scene content can be made visible especially in situations, where sensors of other modalities face issues like a visual-optical camera that needs a source of illumination. As a consequence, not only human mistakes can be avoided by increasing the level of automation, but also machine-induced errors can be reduced that, for example, could make a self-driving car crash into a pedestrian under difficult illumination conditions. Furthermore, multi-spectral sensor systems with infrared imagery as one modality are a rich source of information and can provably increase the robustness of many autonomous systems. Applications that can benefit from utilizing infrared imagery range from robotics to automotive and from biometrics to surveillance. In this book, we provide a brief yet concise introduction to the current state-of-the-art of computer vision and machine learning in the infrared spectrum. Based on various popular computer vision tasks such as image enhancement, object detection, or object tracking, we first motivate each task starting from established literature in the visual-optical spectrum. Then, we discuss the differences between processing images and videos in the visual-optical spectrum and the various infrared spectra. An overview of the current literature is provided together with an outlook for each task. Furthermore, available and annotated public datasets and common evaluation methods and metrics are presented. In a separate chapter, popular applications that can greatly benefit from the use of infrared imagery as a data source are presented and discussed. Among them are automatic target recognition, video surveillance, or biometrics including face recognition. Finally, we conclude with recommendations for well-fitting sensor setups and data processing algorithms for certain computer vision tasks. We address this book to prospective researchers and engineers new to the field but also to anyone who wants to get introduced to the challenges and the approaches of computer vision using infrared images or videos. Readers will be able to start their work directly after reading the book supported by a highly comprehensive backlog of recent and relevant literature as well as related infrared datasets including existing evaluation frameworks. Together with consistently decreasing costs for infrared cameras, new fields of application appear and make computer vision in the infrared spectrum a great opportunity to face nowadays scientific and engineering challenges.

# KEYWORDS

computer vision, infrared, image processing, machine learning, deep learning, thermal, IR, multi-spectral, cross-spectral, datasets, metrics

# Contents

CHAPTER 1

# Introduction

This book provides a brief review of recent efforts in the computer vision and machine learning community to leverage infrared sensing capabilities. Its primary objective is to offer readers an up-to-date summary of applied computer vision techniques to various infrared benchmarking datasets. In this introductory chapter we provide first a brief background of infrared sensing, then we introduce the infrared spectrum along with illustrations of each imaging modality, and finally we conclude this chapter with an overview of the book organization.

## 1.1    INFRARED SENSING: BACKGROUND

The *invisible rays* that cause heat (also known as *dark heat* or *infrared radiation*) were discovered around the year 1800 by astronomer Sir William Herschel. This discovery was first leveraged in 1929 by Britain's scientists, who developed the first infrared-sensitive electronic camera for an anti-aircraft defense system. Nowadays, about 100 years later we perceive our environment with high-quality cooled thermal infrared cameras that are able to sense temperature differences within the observed scene in the range of a few millikelvin. This technology enables us to make camouflaged objects visible at night and to analyze the vascular network of a human face without any active sensing or artificial illumination. At the same time, our everyday life is becoming more and more automated and the development of self-driving cars will soon reach its final stage. Unfortunately, fatal accidents of such autonomous systems still occur due to technical mistakes in the environmental perception. As a result, the utilization of thermal infrared cameras is debated as must-have in the sensor suite of autonomous vehicles to provide the machine learning-based perception engine distinguishable views of vulnerable objects such as pedestrians and cyclists from the static background. Figure 1.1 shows an example of a scene in a typical automotive environment with a cyclist at night acquired by a visual-optical camera and a thermal infrared camera.

In 1992, the U.S. government declassified its infrared imaging technology after being strictly used in military systems, triggering continuous technological advancements up-to-date in infrared light emitters, infrared sensing hardware, and infrared imagery data exploitation for various commercial and industrial applications including security, firefighting, law enforcement, transportation, assistive technologies, advanced driver assistance systems, autonomous driving systems, biometrics, night vision, and medical applications. The first invented LED during the fall of 1961 at Texas Instruments was in fact a near infrared LED emitting at 900 nm wavelength. Such active near infrared illuminators are nowadays key components of widely used eye gaze

Figure 1.1: Sensing in infrared (right) makes moving obstacles (e.g., cyclists) in a driving scenario highly distinguishable from background compared to visual imagery (left).

tracking systems for eye-typing in speech-generative devices (among many other applications), where a special arrangement of LEDs near the optical axis of the infrared camera would produce dark/bright pupils and reflections (glint) off the cornea, making eye gaze tracking devices very accurate down to less than 0.5° error [1]. The reflectance and absorbance of near infrared wavelengths by various surfaces and materials produce a spectroscopic resolution (Fig. 1.2) enabling for instance to distinguish between healthy vs. non-healthy crops (e.g., precision agriculture), Alfalfa plant vs. green vegetation, and dry soil vs. wet soil.

## 1.2   THE INFRARED SPECTRUM

As human beings, our visual perception is dominated by reflected light within a wavelength between 370 and 730 nm of the electromagnetic spectrum [2]. This wavelength range is also called the visual-optical (VIS) spectrum. VIS sensitive cameras capture the visible light either separately in three channel Red-Green-Blue (RGB) color images or entirely in gray-value images [3]. Such cameras are widely used in the field of computer vision, in which acquired images and videos are automatically processed usually in order to enhance or analyze their content for various applications [4, 5]. Seeing or capturing reflected light, however, indicates that a source of illumination is present such as the sun or artificial lighting [6]. When leaving the VIS spectrum toward the longer wavelengths, the infrared (IR) spectrum is adjacent to the VIS but much broader ranging from .73 to 1,000 μm. IR is composed of several spectral bands with different properties, as shown in Table 1.1. Although the human eye cannot see IR light, there are specific cameras that can capture IR radiation. Cameras sensitive to the near infrared (NIR) and short-wave infrared (SWIR) bands that are close to the VIS spectrum capture reflected radiation, too, while mid-wave infrared (MWIR) and long-wave infrared (LWIR) cameras are mostly sensitive to emitted radiation. This emitted radiation originates from all objects in our

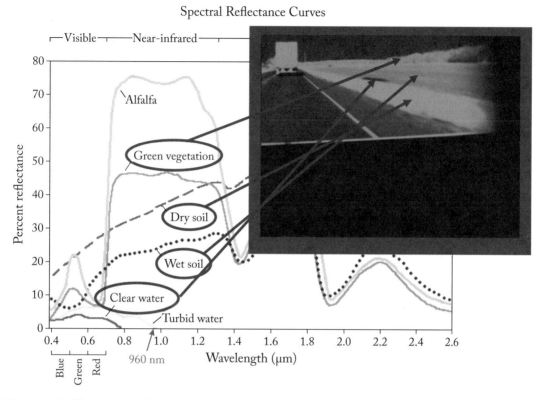

Figure 1.2: Illustration of spectroscopic resolution in near infrared, where the reflectance and absorption of infrared rays generate unique spectral profiles of sensed materials like dry soil, wet soil, green vegetation, and concrete.

everyday world with temperatures above absolute zero and its intensity depends on temperature and material [7]. Temperature differences can be measured in the MWIR and LWIR bands and imaging sensors sensitive to these spectra are also called thermal IR cameras. The main advantage of thermal imaging is that no illumination is needed and hence such cameras can be used for purely passive sensing during day and night.

The atmosphere, namely $CO_2$ and $H_2O$ molecules, can absorb electromagnetic radiation leading to decreasing sensor signal with increasing observation distance [9]. Figure 1.3 shows the transmittance of the atmosphere for wavelengths ranging from the VIS to the LWIR spectrum. There are wavelength ranges such as 5.5–7.5 µm, in which the atmosphere absorbs most of the radiation. This is the reason, why IR cameras are usually not sensitive to the entire wavelengths shown in Table 1.1, but to certain atmospheric windows [10, 11] such as 3–5 µm for MWIR and 8–12 µm for LWIR cameras. Expected ranges for IR cameras can then be predicted on a theoretical basis using radiometric approaches as described by [12]. Some authors use the term

Table 1.1: The different electromagnetic light spectra considered in this book

| Spectrum | Abbreviation | Wavelength | Dominant Radiation |
|---|---|---|---|
| visual-optical | VIS | .37–.73 μm | reflected |
| near infrared | NIR | .73–1.4 μm | reflected |
| short-wave infrared | SWIR | 1.4–3 μm | reflected |
| mid-wave infrared | MWIR | 3–8 μm | emitted |
| long-wave infrared | LWIR | 8–15 μm | emitted |
| far infrared | FIR | 15–1,000 μm | emitted |

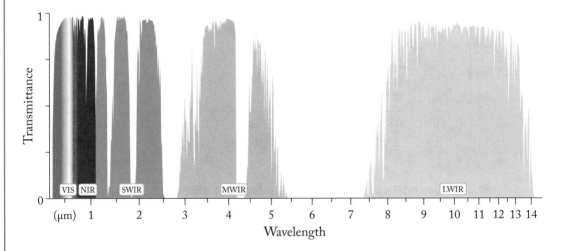

Figure 1.3: Wavelength-specific transmittance of radiation going though 1 km horizontal air path at sea level [8]. *Atmospheric windows* are wavelength ranges with high transmittance. IR cameras are made sensitive to these windows for efficient long-range sensing.

far infrared (FIR) for LWIR cameras [13–15], but in this book we denote such cameras as LWIR cameras only.

The appearance of observed humans, objects, and scenes captured in an image varies greatly across the different spectra, as seen in Fig. 1.4. Further comparative sample images are presented for example in [16], [17], and [18]. Even within the same spectral band, we can observe a strong variation in the appearance of humans or man-made objects depending on season, time, or weather conditions [19]. Since each IR imaging device is focused on one spectral band in general, the resulting image is monochromatic, i.e., there are no color channels such as red, green, and blue in the VIS spectrum. The spectral bands close to VIS such as NIR and SWIR

Figure 1.4: Example images showing the same scene acquired by a VIS, NIR, MWIR, and LWIR camera [15].

are dominated by reflected light and thus usually provide similar imaged information about object and scene textures depending, however, on the observed material: [17] show an example, in which the texture of a metal is clearly visible in the VIS but disappears in the NIR spectrum. NIR and SWIR cameras in contrast to VIS are less sensitive to illumination changes, shading [20], and fog or dust [21]. Within the range of the thermal IR spectra that are dominated by emitted radiation, there is a similarity between object and scene appearance in MWIR and LWIR images. Since many objects emit thermal radiation homogeneously, images are less textured compared to VIS, NIR, and SWIR. This is especially the case for uncooled thermal IR cameras that are less sensitive to temperature differences compared to cooled IR cameras. Objects

Figure 1.5: Two images of the same scene acquired by a VIS and a LWIR camera [15]. Reflected light makes VIS cameras sensitive to texture, while LWIR cameras sense emitted radiation that makes equally tempered texture appear homogeneous.

warmer than their surrounding environment appear bright in the image and with high-quality thermal cameras, even small temperature differences can be sensed such as engine pipes or vascular networks under the human skin. In accordance with [22], it can be stated that textures can be distinguished better in the spectra dominated by reflected radiation and temperature differences can be sensed more distinctly by thermal IR cameras. An example to underline this statement is given in Fig. 1.5. Just like many new technologies, IR cameras were first introduced to military applications such as night vision, armored vehicle detection and identification, missile approach warning, or target tracking [6]. Due to the decreasing costs within the last 10–20 years paired with increasing imaging quality and resolution, many new applications emerged [7]. They range from material classification, visual inspection, and biometrics for NIR and SWIR cameras to automotive safety, medical examination technology, and surveillance for thermal IR cameras.

The datasets used for evaluation are mainly coming from ground-based cameras that can be either stationary mounted on buildings or mobile mounted on any kind of robot or vehicle. As a result, surveillance and automotive datasets dominate the dataset collections introduced in this book. However, some aerial video data acquired by manned aircraft or Unmanned Aerial Vehicles (UAVs) is discussed, too. The NIR spectrum and the thermal IR bands are currently the most popular ones in IR computer vision. While NIR is adjacent to the VIS spectrum and can usually be captured by standard cameras, thermal IR cameras are popular as they can complement VIS cameras as an orthogonal source of passively sensed data. Hence, those kind of data is represented most across the chapters of this book.

# 1.3    BOOK ORGANIZATION

As IR sensors usually have lower resolution and higher noise level compared to visual imagery, we dedicate Chapter 2 to the topic of infrared image enhancement and super resolution. We discuss techniques to handle noise and weak contrast that can remain in the image as artifacts after the imaging process. Furthermore, we focus on long-range sensing and present methods to mitigate atmospheric effects such as haze or turbulence. From the spectral point of view, this chapter is rather dominated by thermal IR imagery. In Chapter 3, we present cross-spectral image processing, where one spectral band usually supplements or guides another to solve a certain task more robustly or to make images easier to interpret for humans. Such tasks are for example image registration and alignment as well as cross-spectral colorization. The spectral bands considered in this chapter greatly vary as there are multiple ways for a cross-spectral combination of different spectra. Multi-spectral computer vision approaches, which utilize multiple spectral bands that are pixel accurately aligned and process them equally weighted, are directly discussed in the related chapter. In Chapter 4, we review recent literature on infrared imagery exploitation. Various popular computer vision tasks are discusses such as object detection, classification, and tracking. Each topic is motivated coming from the rather traditional VIS computer vision. Then, the reader is introduced to the similarities of and the differences between VIS and IR from the image processing point of view. Recent machine and deep learning-based techniques are presented and described to understand the difference between Deep Convolutional Neural Networks (DCNNs) that process VIS or IR images. Then, traditional and modern applications such as video surveillance or biometrics are presented in Chapter 5. We do see a tendency that most of this chapter's sections again predominantly discuss thermal IR imagery. However, especially in face recognition the literature rather relies on spectra that are dominated by reflected light such as VIS, NIR, or SWIR. Those spectral bands seem to contain the more important information and more powerful features. Finally, we conclude the book in Chapter 6 with a brief summary and recommend sensors for certain applications to prospective researchers and engineers.

# CHAPTER 2

# Image and Video Enhancement

Image and video enhancement aims at improving the signal quality relative to imaging artifacts such as noise and blur or atmospheric perturbations such as turbulence and haze. It is usually performed in order to assist humans in analyzing image and video content or simply to present humans visually appealing images and videos. However, image and video enhancement can also be used as a preprocessing technique to ease the task and thus improve the performance of subsequent automatic image content analysis algorithms: preceding dehazing can improve object detection as shown by [23] or explicit turbulence modeling can improve moving object detection as discussed by [24]. But it remains an open question whether image and video enhancement should rather be performed explicitly as a preprocessing step or implicitly for example by feeding affected images directly to a neural network for image content analysis like object detection [25]. Especially for real-time video processing at low latency it can be better to handle image perturbation implicitly in order to minimize the processing time of an algorithm. This can be achieved by making algorithms for image content analysis robust or even invariant to perturbations such as noise or blur. Additionally, mistakes of an individual preprocessing module can obviously affect the quality of the entire processing pipeline.

An important aspect of image enhancement is Image Quality Assessment (IQA). The question is: can we define metrics that help us to objectively assess the quality of an image? One example was already given by the work of [23], in which the detection rate of an object detector was improved by preceding dehazing. But if we want to be task-agnostic, how can we assess the quality in a generic way? This topic actually is a large field of research on its own. Two main approaches can be identified: (1) full-reference IQA, where we need a reference image (= ground truth) for a comparison with the enhanced image. The measures work best if the images are precisely aligned; and (2) no-reference or blind IQA, where no reference image is needed and the image quality is assessed just from the enhanced image. Obviously, blind IQA measures are more powerful than full-reference, but also very difficult to obtain. Here, we briefly review both approaches in order to understand how image quality can be measured. In general, Natural Scene Statistics (NSS) serve as a basis for IQA [26]. The assumption is that the human perceptual system is designed to interpret scenes and therefore needs to observe statistical regularities within the scenes. Full-reference IQA [27] is in general more popular since well-established and intuitive measures exist such as Mean Squared Error (MSE), Root-Mean-Square Error

(RMSE), and Peak-Signal-To-Noise Ratio (PSNR) [28] as well as Structural Similarity (SSIM) and Multi-Scale SSIM [29]. Approaches based on information theory like the Visual Information Fidelity (VIF) [30] are common evaluation measures. For blind IQA, popular measures are based on NSS, and mostly tackle certain scene properties, which is also called distortion-specific IQA. Such measures are for example Blind/Referenceless Image Spatial QUality Evaluator (BRISQUE) [31], Natural Image Quality Evaluator (NIQE) [32], or Learned Perceptual Image Patch Similarity (LPIPS) [33] for single images and Video Multi-Method Assessment Fusion (VMAF)[1] or VIDeo quality EVALuator (VIDEVAL) [34] for videos. They measure different properties such as naturalness of the scene or the expected dominant frequencies in an image. The mentioned IQA measures are originally designed for VIS images, of course. Rather generic measures that do not rely too much on NSS such as MSE, PSNR, or SSIM can be adopted for IR IQA. [35] analyzes NSS for LWIR images and states that there are statistical regularities similar to VIS images. BRISQUE for example can be applied to LWIR images, when using a different parameterization. Furthermore, LWIR specific properties such as non-uniformity or halo effects can be measured.

In this chapter, we will not analyze the IR imaging process itself. This means that we will not discuss topics like Non-Uniformity Correction (NUC) [36], defective pixel correction [37], tone mapping [38], image compression, camera calibration, or the correction of lens distortion. Instead, we focus on approaches to correct remaining imaging artifacts such as noise or weak contrast and to mitigate atmospheric perturbations like fog, haze, or turbulence. In a separate section, we discuss approaches for super resolution as this is one of the most prominent techniques for enhancing IR images. The reason is obvious: IR cameras are still much more expensive compared to VIS cameras and one of the price boosters is image resolution. With a super resolution algorithm, the physical resolution of the imaging device can be magnified digitally after image acquisition. As a result, super resolution is a popular method to overcome the issue of low IR image resolution.

There are several similarities between enhancement for VIS and IR images and videos. This is the case especially for NIR and SWIR images with an appearance that is rather close to the VIS spectrum. However, in this chapter we aim at emphasizing the differences that arise when enhancing IR image in general, which also includes thermal IR. These differences can be camera specific noise models or the sensitivity of IR cameras to certain perturbations.

## 2.1    DENOISING AND CONTRAST ENHANCEMENT

When looking at an image as a human or a machine, high image quality is important for any kind of task [39]. This image quality can be characterized by showing the observed scene's content clearly and with well visible details such as edges, textures, and structures. At the same time, effects that degrade the image quality such as noise or weak contrast shall be minimized as they disturb the image content analysis. This applies to both VIS and IR images. The reality, however,

---

[1]https://github.com/Netflix/vmaf (last accessed: August 15, 2021).

shows that during the imaging process there is no way to avoid such undesired effects despite the great progress achieved in optimizing the quality and performance of imaging devices in recent years. Multiple sources can affect the image quality: cameras produce different kinds of electrical noise like for example readout noise, photon noise, or thermal noise (= dark noise). Actually, an image is usually influenced by a superposition of different types of noise that underlie different noise models and occur at different levels. In the past, a variety of models was developed such as Gaussian, Poisson, speckle, or Salt-and-Pepper in order to model noise on the one hand and to design filters for denoising on the other hand [40]. In [41], a comprehensive overview of the topic is provided.

But how exactly does noise affect the image? The pixel values undergo a shift that can be additive (e.g., Gaussian), multiplicative (e.g., speckle), or impulsive (e.g., Salt-and-Pepper). Often, the occurrence of noise is not spatio-temporally consistent, i.e., pixel positions and values affected by noise vary randomly over time. One exception is fixed-pattern noise that originates from the imaging device's pixel-wise different efficiencies in the capture of radiation and thus is spatially and temporally constant [41]. As image denoising is one of the traditional image processing tasks, there is a vast number of publications available. Brief overviews of the recent state-of-the-art for VIS images are provided by [42] and [43]. Video denoising with its temporal dimension offers more opportunities for denoising but is less explored in the literature [44, 45]. The denoising approaches range from simple image filtering using Gaussian or median filters to complex, edge-preserving filtering techniques [46, 47]. Temporal filtering via pixel-wise median or averaging is a powerful approach for video denoising as it can well utilize the random characteristic of noise. Furthermore, very interesting deep learning-based approaches for model-blind denoising were published recently, where camera specific noise is learned implicitly and unsupervised by a DCNN just from example videos [48, 49]. Obviously, this works for random noise only and not for fixed-pattern noise. One additional drawback at this time is the need for precise calculation of optical flow to estimate each pixel's motion between consecutive frames. Even more recent methods overcome this drawback and learn image denoising by adding noise to a noisy image [50] and train a DCNN with the original noisy image as pseudo label in a self-supervised learning manner [51]. The discussed deep learning-based approaches are applicable to VIS and IR cameras likewise and show impressive results.

When exploring the differences between VIS and IR cameras regarding the presence of noise, we can actually discover many similarities [52]. The types of noise do not differ significantly but the mixture of noise apparent in the resulting image is different: thermal noise for example affects thermal IR sensors stronger than VIS sensors [53]. This is specifically the case for uncooled microbolometers [54]. The well-known impulse noise that is often linked to IR imagery [55] seems to be not as representative [54]. The reason might be that impulse noise can model dead pixels of the sensor well, but modern IR cameras are equipped with appropriate embedded pre-processing algorithms that detect and correct dead pixels automatically. In general, we can use the same denoising techniques in both the VIS and the IR spectrum.

This means that Gaussian or median filters are popular tools for fast and generic denoising and more complex methods such as a bilateral filter can be used to preserve edges and receive better image quality at higher computational costs. For IR images, however, preserving the edges can be even more important compared to VIS images as image resolution is still a highly limiting and expensive factor for IR cameras. Furthermore, since long-range IR cameras often observe objects in a distance of several kilometers, those objects can have a tiny appearance in the image and hence it is crucial to avoid any blurring of the object boundaries during denoising. Other authors propose to use wavelet transform [56], non-local means filtering [57], or adaptive mean shift [58] for object structure preserving denoising of IR images. One specific type of noise that deserves further attention in the context of IR imaging is fixed-pattern noise. It occurs due to the uneven response of the individual pixels and has the appearance of a spatially constant grid often with horizontal and/or vertical stripes [59]. It is also called non-uniformity noise and the non-uniformity correction [36], which is a pre-processing algorithm usually embedded in the imaging device, is supposed to suppress this kind of noise. The remaining noise, however, can appear especially in scenarios with low contrast. Over time, fixed-pattern noise spatially drifts, which makes its reduction even more challenging [60]. Assuming that fixed-pattern noise only occurs as vertical stripes, horizontal smoothing along the image rows is proposed [61]. All presented methods up to now just consider single IR images. A deep learning-based approach is proposed in [60]: real thermal IR images are corrupted with artificial fixed-pattern noise to train a scene adaptive DCNN. Finally, one of the few IR video denoising approaches is presented in [62]: using spatio-temporal filtering, random and fixed-pattern noise can be reduced jointly.

In addition to noise, weak contrast is another unwanted image property and can be the result of insufficient illumination for VIS, NIR, and SWIR cameras or the absence of temperature differences for SWIR, MWIR, and LWIR cameras. Another reason for weak contrast can be atmospheric effects like haze or fog. Those are discussed later in Section 2.2. Figure 2.1 shows example VIS and LWIR image pairs taken from the KAIST Multispectral Pedestrian Detection Benchmark Dataset [63]. The daylight scene shows a situation with good visibility in the VIS spectrum and degraded visibility in the IR spectrum due to a lack of relative temperature differences across the scene. The person wearing a red shirt is clearly visible in the VIS spectrum (green arrow) but not in the LWIR spectrum (red arrow). In the nighttime scene, however, the conditions are vice versa. Due to the lack of illumination, the VIS camera cannot see the humans on the sidewalk and on the street (red arrows) but the IR camera can clearly see the humans (green arrows) as the generally lower temperature at night causes an increased temperature difference between scene and objects. Just like denoising, contrast enhancement is one of the standard and most prominent image processing tasks. And again, similar approaches can be applied for contrast enhancement in the VIS and the IR spectrum. Traditional and well-known approaches are Histogram Equalization (HE), Adaptive Histogram Equalization (AHE), or Contrast Limited Adaptive Histogram Equalization (CLAHE) that are described, for exam-

Figure 2.1: Two VIS and LWIR image pairs taken from the KAIST Multispectral Pedestrian Detection Benchmark [63] showing weak contrast in VIS images due to insufficient illumination at nighttime and in IR images due to similar scene temperature at daytime. Pedestrians marked with an arrow are easy to spot in one spectrum (green color) but difficult to spot in the other spectrum (red color).

ple in [64]. The mentioned approaches except for HE operate locally, i.e., the input image is tiled and each tile is processed separately. In this way, a local image region can be contrast enhanced even if the related local contrast does not contribute much to the global image contrast and hence global image contrast enhancement would consider this region only weakly. To avoid tiling artifacts, averaging is performed at the seams. If not applied carefully, histogram equalization can amplify noise. As a consequence, contrast enhancement is often performed jointly with denoising [65]. A rather early but important work on contrast enhancement for IR images is presented in [66]: with the assumption that thermal IR images are piecewise constant, a spatial and a spatiotemporal homomorphic filter is proposed. Another specific property of IR images in certain applications is that objects of interest can appear very small in the image. Naïve histogram equalization can then lead to an undesired reduction of the signal in image regions containing those objects. In [67], a histogram based equalization method is adapted and extended in order to preserve the appearance of small objects in the image. The same challenge is tackled in [68] using adaptive histogram segmentation and local contrast weighted distributions. In [69], the entropy is calculated to measure the detail level of local image regions. Then, the multi-scale tophat transform is used for contrast enhancement preserving small objects and fine details. In [70], the authors build up on CLAHE but use neighborhood conditional histograms instead to give greater weight to pixel values in detailed image regions and thus to avoid the over-enhancement of homogeneous image regions. Global and local histogram-based contrast enhancement methods guided by edge information are combined in [71]. Finally, in [72], the authors use a DCNN trained for joint denoising and super resolution.

At this time, we do not know about any public dataset that is specifically dedicated to IR image enhancement. We would expect such a dataset to come with real images that provide both good quality and bad quality and that can be directly compared using standard metrics. Therefore, aligned images showing the same scene under different challenging conditions must be provided. Recently, a dataset for super resolution was released [73], but this topic is discussed individually later in Section 2.3. In order to provide a quantitative evaluation in addition to the qualitative evaluation, most authors artificially degrade images using known noise models such as Gaussian or Poisson. This is actually the same for authors active in VIS and IR imagery. Typical measures are PSNR and SSIM. Some authors [68, 71] add further metrics like Measure of Enhancement by Entropy (EMEE), No-Reference Structural Sharpness (NRSS), Lightness Order Error (LOE), Logarithmic Michelson Contrast Measure (AME), or linear index of fuzziness to measure specific image properties such as contrast, blur, entropy, or sharpness. If those measures are more suitable for IR images compared to the ones mentioned in the introduction of this chapter remains an open question. We do see many IQA measures in the literature, however, which indicates the importance of this topic.

## 2.2   MITIGATING ATMOSPHERIC PERTURBATIONS

The atmosphere contributes crucially to the quality of the acquired images. Electromagnetic radiation gets absorbed or scattered on its way through the atmosphere and thus less electromagnetic radiant energy reaches the imaging device. Scattering is complex phenomenon, however, as it comprises effects like reflection, refraction, or diffraction in different levels and variations. A detailed description of scattering and radiation transfer in general is given in [74]. Obviously, with a growing distance between camera and scene, the atmosphere increasingly makes the image quality degrade. Nevertheless, the composition of the atmosphere plays an important role: depending on the size of the present particles, some spectral bands are scattered stronger than others as stated in [75]. Large particles such as water droplets or ice crystals affect radiation energy in the VIS and the IR spectrum likewise. A similar observation can be made for particles with a size similar to the wavelength being scattered such as dust, water vapor, or pollen. This effect is called *Mie scattering*. Probably the most interesting type of scattering in the context of this book is called *Raleigh scattering* caused by particles much smaller than the wavelength of the scattered radiation such as oxygen or nitrogen molecules for example. Due to the shorter wavelength of the VIS spectrum, VIS cameras are affected stronger by Raleigh scattering than IR cameras. Raleigh scattering leads to the well-known example of a scene that can be observed well with a SWIR camera while a VIS camera captures nothing but haze [9]. It can be shown that SWIR cameras achieve better performance under such conditions for both observation by humans [76] and computer vision tasks like person detection [77]. Unfortunately, depending on the local composition of the atmosphere, fog, dust, or smoke particles can be large enough to scatter longer wavelengths, too, and hence this potential benefit of IR cameras can be gone for the acquired images at the end.

From the physics point of view this seems to be a pity, but this gives us as computer vision scientists the chance to utilize traditional algorithm engineering or novel machine learning techniques in order to reduce or correct the influence of the atmosphere. In images and videos, the described phenomenon leads to reduced visibility of scene content especially at remote locations. *Dehazing* is a well-known method to remove haze, smoke, dust, or fog from single images without any prior knowledge about the camera, calibration data, scene content, 3D structure, or environmental conditions [78]. A quite old but still very popular formulation of the problem is given in [79]:

$$I(\mathbf{x}) = t(\mathbf{x})J(\mathbf{x}) + (1 - t(\mathbf{x}))A \qquad (2.1)$$

In this physical modeling of haze affected image acquisition, the hazy image $I$ is composed by the haze-free image $J$ and the medium transmission $t$ at each pixel position $\mathbf{x}$ as well as the constant color vector $A$ called atmospheric light. $t$ ranges from 0–1 for each pixel and describes the amount of light that reaches the imaging device. Furthermore, $t$ is inversely related to the scene's depth. The term $(1 - t(\mathbf{x}))A$ is called airlight and represents the potential shift of colors in the scene originating from different sources of illumination in addition to the sunlight.

Equation 2.1 is originally defined on the three-channel RGB color space, which indicates that it may not be suitable for dehazing IR images. Before we discuss this question, we briefly review the existing approaches for dehazing RGB color images. Probably the most popular approach is dehazing using the Dark Channel Prior (DCP), as proposed in [80]. The assumption is that within each image patch, at least one color channel has an intensity close to zero. From this so-called dark channel, the thickness of the haze can be estimated and used to recover the haze-free image. Another popular and elegant approach uses the non-local prior [81], where it is assumed that only a few hundred distinct colors exist and that they are smeared across the RGB space due to the presence of haze. These colors can be clustered and represented by haze-lines that then can be used for reconstructing the haze-free image. Deep learning, of course, offered new opportunities for dehazing and impressive results were achieved recently using DCNNs [82, 83]. The problem of having training data with haze-free images serving as ground truth was solved by adding synthetic haze artificially to real images [23, 84]. Additionally, a novel dataset containing real hazy and haze-free images was released by Ancuti et al. [85] recently. A recommendable overview of dehazing and its current state-of-the-art is given in [23].

Dehazing monochromatic IR images is a not as easy as we cannot use the above mentioned assumptions. The described approaches, however, can be utilized for dehazing cross-, multi-, and hyperspectral images as we will show in Section 3.3. But there is another technique that has been successfully applied to dehaze color images and that can be adopted for IR images: *Retinex*. Retinex theory was originally introduced in [86] as a color vision model of human perception. The term is a contraction of retina and cortex. According to [87], Retinex can be seen as a *theoretical spectral channel that makes spatial comparisons between scene regions so as to calculate Lightness sensations*. Therefore, three independent spatial color channels were introduced that later were mapped to the camera color space RGB to set a basis for multiple different image enhancement techniques such as color restoration, shadow removal, or contrast enhancement [88, 89]. Among them is dehazing as described very intuitively and concisely by [90]. So, this means we are still talking about dehazing color images but in contrast to the approaches described before, Retinex can be successfully applied to the luminance channel only and hence to intensity images, too, as we usually have them in IR image processing. The basic idea is to assume that the image is hazy and to estimate the scene's depth (or transmissivity) from the different frequencies and related amplitudes present in the image using multi-scale Retinex [91, 92]. The haze can then be estimated locally from the lower image frequencies. Comparable approaches were proposed in different variations by multiple authors [93–95]. An important paper in this context was published in [96], who show that Eq. (2.1) is suitable for gray-value images, too, and that estimating the scene's atmospheric veil (= airlight) can be done similarly for color images using the DCP or for gray-value images using (multi-scale Retinex-like) image smoothing. Finally, it should be mentioned that DCP-based dehazing and Retinex are a well-matching combination to further improve the dehazing result [97]. However, we do not see any related work specifically for IR images and videos in the literature up to now. The reason could be that the approach expects well-textured images. Only rather expensive cameras are able to acquire such images like, for example, SWIR cameras or actively cooled thermal IR cameras. But authors of currently available datasets did either not use such high-quality cameras or tackle different tasks such as face recognition without the presence of haze. Other approaches incorporate separately determined depth information [98] to overcome the need for color information or learn handling difficult environmental condition implicitly for certain tasks such as person detection [99]. Unfortunately, currently no public datasets exist for dehazing with IR images and videos to the best of the authors' knowledge. Just a dataset for person detection under difficult weather conditions called UNIRI-TID is available [100].

Besides the composition of the atmosphere, we also want to address the phenomenon of atmospheric turbulence [101]. In the context of this book, atmospheric turbulence denotes heat

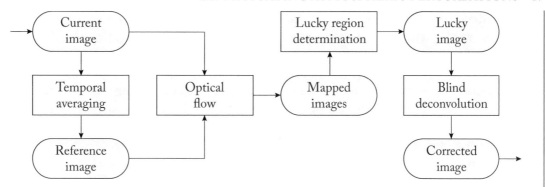

Figure 2.2: Typical processing pipeline for turbulence mitigation.

shimmer also known as heat haze. Such turbulence can occur regularly for a long-range imaging device mounted near the ground observing a scene in a distance of several kilometers. It is an atmospheric effect caused by temporally variable streak formation due to rising air layers of different temperature, and thus different air density, over surfaces hotter than the surrounding air. Within a video, turbulence appears as temporally and spatially variable wobble and can severely disturb the user's view of the scene. Other authors describe the visual effects as spatio-temporally varying random shifts [102], local deformations [24], or warping and blurring [103]. While dehazing can be applied to single images and videos likewise, turbulence mitigation implicitly includes the temporal dimension. This means we focus on video processing in the remainder of this section. In order to provide a steady image, algorithms are discussed to mitigate turbulence. Both the VIS and the IR spectrum are affected similarly by atmospheric turbulence.

According to [104], the currently most common approach for turbulence mitigation consists of the following steps: (1) calculations of a reference image, (2) calculation of the optical flow between reference and current image, (3) determination of the so-called lucky region, and (4) deconvolution. An overview of this approach is depicted in Fig. 2.2. Pixel-wise temporal averaging is the most popular method to calculate a reference frame [104–106]. In this way, the stationary parts of the scene are expected to be stabilized despite the turbulence. Incoming images are then mapped to this reference image using optical flow [106, 107]. The blur still remains in the mapped image as it is spatially varying. From a set of mapped images, we individually pick the sharpest regions (= lucky regions) to create the lucky image. Assuming that the current image was recovered from the turbulence except for the diffraction limited blur, blind deconvolution can be used to correct the remaining blur. Therefore, methods like total variation [107] or Wiener deconvolution [106] can be applied. But even a rather simple approach like unsharp masking [102] can be promising especially when the calculation has to be fast. As recently discussed in [108], deep learning-based methods have not established themselves for turbulence mitigation, yet, as they lack in implicitly handling different strength levels of turbulence. But this may be a drawback of the turbulence simulator that was used to generate the training data. Instead, it can be more promising to use deep learning and DCNNs just for specific steps of the processing pipeline like the blind deconvolution as proposed by [102].

The approach described above works well if the scene is static. This means there is a stationary background and no moving objects appear. The calculation of the reference image is severely disturbed and affected by smearing artifacts if this assumption is violated by a moving camera or by the presence of moving objects in the scene. In that case, camera motion can be compensated by image registration and alignment before calculating the reference image. Object motion, however, must be handled explicitly: motion segmentation [24, 109] is one option but often suffers from hardly observable and thus not precisely determinable object boundaries. Another option is dynamic turbulence mitigation [110] that uses optical flow to estimate motion for both camera and objects locally in the image. A third option is using an object detector [111] that, however, works only if the expected object classes are known prior and if the moving object's appearance allows a robust detection.

Although the literature on turbulence is quite rich, there is not much related work on specific turbulence mitigation for IR cameras [24, 103, 112]. But as already mentioned, the approaches presented can be similarly applied to VIS and IR video data of all spectra. As a consequence, several authors do not distinguish between the spectra and simply use VIS and IR data simultaneously for their experiments [107, 110, 113]. Some authors combine turbulence mitigation with approaches for motion segmentation or moving object detection [24, 109, 110], dehazing [114], or super resolution [113] to solve multiple tasks simultaneously.

A short survey on turbulence mitigation, dataset acquisition, and an unfortunately anonymous comparison of current approaches is given in [115]. Besides the standard full-reference IQA metrics PSNR or SSIM, other metrics were proposed to measure the quality of turbulence mitigation. [116] use the blur and the tilt measures: the mean blur of each input and output image is calculated and averaged across the sequence. For the tilt measure, the motion between frames is calculated and represented as averaged pixel-wise shift vectors. For a properly working turbulence mitigation algorithm, both measures are expected to be lower for the output images compared to the input. Another metric called Turbulence Mitigation Metric (TMM) was introduced by [114]: the assumption is that an image sequence after turbulence mitigation is more temporally consistent than before. Therefore, this temporal consistency is calculated for the input and the output sequence separately and then the two values are compared. The only public IR dataset known to the authors that is affected by turbulence is the SENSIAC ATR Database[2] that unfortunately does not come with a ground truth regarding turbulence mitigation.

---

[2]https://www.dsiac.org/resources/available-databases/atr-algorithm-development-image-database (last accessed: August 23, 2021).

# 2.3    SUPER RESOLUTION

The usage of IR images has been increasing during the last two decades, in particular thermal imagery due to the reduction of costs and availability of thermal cameras [6]. However, in spite of the continuous increase on the usage of thermal cameras, there is still the limitation on image resolution. This limitation is imposed by the technology needed in the thermal cameras. Although there are some high-resolution thermal cameras on the market, they are generally based on a more expensive technology—actively cooled thermal cameras; hence, most of the applications are based on utilizing uncooled thermal cameras, which are available on the market at a significantly lower price.

In order to overcome the resolution limitation mentioned above, Super Resolution (SR) techniques, initially intended for the visual-optical spectrum, can be adapted to work in the thermal domain—both, traditional algorithm-based [117, 118] and machine learning-based [119, 120] SR methods can be considered. SR approaches try to recover a High Resolution (HR) image from one or more Low Resolution (LR) input images. In general, traditional approaches tackle the SR problem in a multi-image framework [121, 122], which is also called Multi-Frame Super Resolution (MFSR). A set of LR images of the same scene with sub-pixel shifts are considered as input. MFSR is usually formulated as an ill-posed problem [121], where the HR image is degraded to the LR image by an unknown source. This unknown source can for instance be modeled by considering a combination of atmosphere blur, motion effect, camera blur, and downsampling. Each LR image imposes a set of linear constraints on the unknown HR intensity values. If enough LR images are available (at subpixel misalignment), then the set of equations becomes determined and can be solved to recover the HR image. This framework is physically limited to small increases in resolution: usually just up to ×2 scaled HR images are obtained. The first work on MFSR was proposed in [123]: it uses the combination of multiple images with subpixel displacements with frequency-domain techniques to improve the spatial resolution. Since then, several spatial domain MFSR techniques were considered (e.g., projection onto convex sets, non-uniform interpolation, sparse coding, regularized methods) and techniques that combines the advantages of multiple images fusion with learning the low- to high-resolution mapping using deep networks have been considered [124, 125]. In order to overcome the upsampling scale limitation some authors have proposed different single-image frameworks [126, 127] that are also known as Single-Frame Super Resolution (SFSR). In general, single-image SR frameworks recover the HR image by means of a set of training examples, they are also referred in the literature to as *example-based single-image SR*. In these approaches, correspondences between low- and high-resolution image patches are learned and then applied to a new LR image to recover its most likely HR version. The performance of these methods is highly dependent on the sample correspondences present in the training data and especially for larger scale magnification such as ×4, SR becomes actually more like an hallucination [128]. Although there are different evaluation techniques to assess SR results [129], in general PSNR and SSIM are considered as quantitative metrics to evaluate performance of different approaches [130].

Applying MFSR techniques to thermal IR images dates back to van Eekeren [117]. This work was intended to obtain SR images of small moving objects against a cluttered background. The proposed solution helps to improve recognition rates of small moving objects. The proposed method can be divided into three parts: (1) the SR representation of the scene's background is estimated; this background is later on used to detect moving objects; (2) the trajectory model of the moving object is computed to obtain a subpixel representation; and (3) the HR representation is obtained by solving an inverse problem. Surprisingly, there is just few literature on MFSR for thermal images, which indicates that approaches adopted from the VIS spectrum seem to be well-suited for IR imagery as well. Recently, a multi-image super-resolution algorithm applied to thermal imagery has been proposed by Mandanici et al. in [131]. This approach is applied to terrestrial thermal imaging to overcome the limitation of the low resolution. Multi-image super-resolution of remotely sensed images using a novel residual feature attention deep neural network has been proposed by Salvetti et al. [132]. It efficiently tackles MFSR tasks, simultaneously exploiting spatial and temporal correlations, to combine multiple images.

In recent years, most of the SR approaches proposed in the literature follow the single-image framework by using deep learning-based techniques since they have shown the most promising results. In general, learning-based approaches follow a supervised scheme, where a DCNN is trained to get an HR image from a given LR one. These schemes are generally trained by downsampling and adding both noise and blur to the given HR image, which is used as a ground truth. This downsampled image used as an input guarantees a pixel-level correspondence after the upsampling process. One of the first DCNN-based thermal IR image SR approach has been introduced by Choi et al. in [133], which is inspired by the proposal in [134] intended for VIS images. [133] compares the accuracy of a network trained in different image spectra to find the best representation of thermal enhancement. As a conclusion, it is shown that a grayscale trained network provides better enhancement than the MWIR-based network for thermal image enhancement. On the contrary to previous approaches, a novel unsupervised scheme is presented in [73] based on the usage of a CycleGAN architecture for thermal IR single-image SR. The unsupervised architecture allows not only to obtain a SR representation from the given LR image, but it also allows to learn how to generate an HR image from a real LR image. Please note that supervised approaches mentioned above are trained by downsampling the given image, which is assumed as the HR ground truth. In other words, LR images used for training supervised approaches are synthesized images, but not real one.

The existing literature focused on the thermal image SR problem has been continuously increasing and novel DCNN-based architectures are proposed every year. The active scientific community was taken as a motivation to define a benchmark—thermal image dataset [73]—to be used in the first Thermal Image Super Resolution (TISR) challenge hold in 2020 during the 17th IEEE Workshop on Perception Beyond the Visible Spectrum (PBVS). This work-

Figure 2.3: Illustration of thermal IR images [73] used in the TISR Challenge at the PBVS workshop [135]: image with 160×120 pixels native resolution from an Axis Domo P1290 (left), image with 320×240 native resolution from an Axis Q2901-E (center), image with 640×480 resolution from an FC-6320 FLIR (native resolution is 640×512) (right).

shop is held annually in conjunction with the IEEE International Conference on Computer Vision and Pattern Recognition (CVPR). The best results from this challenge, 6 teams out of 51 participants, have been published at [135]. Hence, this paper provides a good overview of state-of-the-art in thermal IR image SR. The TISR challenge consists of creating a solution capable of generating a super-resolved thermal IR image in ×2, ×3, and ×4 scales from cameras with different resolutions. This is in contrast to most of the existing SR benchmarks that synthesize LR from HR images by downscaling, which leads to unrealistic LR images, of course. The dataset used in this challenge consists of a set of 1,021 thermal IR images acquired using three different thermal cameras with different resolutions (see Fig. 2.3). The dataset contains images under various lighting conditions such as morning, afternoon, or night, and objects such as buildings, cars, people, or vegetation.

In summary, the IR image SR topic is a quite active research field with a lot of possible solutions to explore, both in the single-image and multi-image frameworks. Although a large number of different architectures have been recently proposed under the deep learning-based paradigm, there is a lot of space for improvement. It should be mentioned that a large number of architectures proposed for the infrared image SR are just adaptations from the visible spectrum domain, hence the design of architectures by using attention mechanisms specifically designed to tackle the infrared imagery is still an open problem.

CHAPTER 3

# CHAPTER 3

# Cross-Spectral Image Processing

Although this book is on IR computer vision and its main focus lies on IR image and video processing and analysis, a special attention is dedicated to cross-spectral image processing due to the increasing number of publications and applications in this domain. In these cross-spectral frameworks, IR information is used together with information from other spectral bands to tackle some specific problems by developing more robust solutions. Tasks considered for cross-spectral processing are for instance dehazing, segmentation, vegetation index estimation, or face recognition. This increasing number of applications is motivated by cross- and multi-spectral camera setups available already on the market like for example smartphones, remote sensing multi-spectral cameras, or multi-spectral cameras for automotive systems or drones. In this chapter, different cross-spectral image processing techniques will be reviewed together with possible applications. Initially, image registration approaches for the cross-spectral case are reviewed: the registration stage is the first image processing task, which is needed to align images acquired by different sensors within the same reference coordinate system. Then, recent cross-spectral image colorization approaches, which are intended to colorize infrared images for different applications are presented. Finally, the cross-spectral image enhancement problem is tackled by including guided super resolution techniques, image dehazing approaches, cross-spectral filtering and edge detection. Figure 3.1 illustrates cross-spectral image processing stages as well as their possible connections. Table 3.1 presents some of the available public cross-spectral datasets generally used as reference data to evaluate cross-spectral image registration, colorization, enhancement, or exploitation results.

## 3.1 IMAGE REGISTRATION

In sensor suites, where cross- or multi-spectral imagery is acquired by different sensors, an image alignment or registration processing step is required to align the information to the same reference coordinate system. Although both terms image *alignment* and *registration* could be indistinctly used to refer to the process of warping images together, the alignment techniques in general only consider rigid transformations (i.e., homographies), while registration includes both rigid and non-rigid transformations needed to geometrically transform images to the same coordinate system [151]—through this section the image registration term will be considered since it is a more general one. Image registration is the first and actually most critical step needed

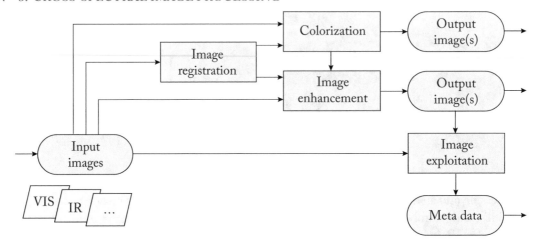

Figure 3.1: Illustration of different cross-spectral image processing stages and possible connections; cross-spectral images can be used both, after a registration stage (supervised training) or as they are provided by the sensors (unsupervised training). Image enhancement can be dehazing, super resolution, or filtering, while image exploitation (see Chapter 5) can be object detection, visual odometry, or semantic segmentation.

to solve further stages. In fact, most of the success of further stages depends on the accuracy of this warping process. Most successful image enhancement and exploitation approaches strongly benefit from pixel-accurate registration. Instead of solving this task using computer vision algorithms, it is possible to choose a sensor setup, in which the image registration task is solved implicitly using for example a beam splitter and precise sensor calibration [63].

Registration and alignment of cross-spectral image pairs is a challenging task as the scene appearance is not only distorted by temporal or spatial deformations, i.e., images have potentially been acquired at different time and point of view, but also look different since images have been acquired by sensors sensitive to different spectral bands. A larger distance in spectral range of the used spectral bands (see Table 1.1) usually leads to a larger difference in scene appearance, which makes the registration task more challenging. The most difficult cross-spectral scenario corresponds to the case of registering VIS and thermal IR images since the appearance of those images strongly differs. There are many potential applications for cross- and multi-spectral images and videos. Some of them will be discussed below and can be considered as extensions to those presented in Chapter 2. Other applications such as image colorization are rather novel and can be tackled only by using such a kind of frameworks based on the usage of heterogeneous information. In all these cases, the content of the provided cross-spectral images is different due to the non-linear intensity variations that usually exist between images from different spectral bands. Furthermore, image content acquired by different cameras from different perspectives and maybe even at different times is affected by translational and rotational offsets,

Table 3.1: Available public cross-spectral datasets. Additional cross-spectral datasets are provided in Tables 4.1, 4.2, and 5.1 ([FLIR-REF]: https://www.flir.com/oem/adas/adas-dataset-form/ (last accessed: April 2, 2021)).

| Dataset | Related Publication | Year | Spectral Bands and Add. Information |
|---|---|---|---|
| ND-Collection X1 | [137] | 2003 | NIR-VIS |
| OSU Color-Thermal Database | [138] | 2007 | LWIR-VIS |
| RGB-NIR Scene Dataset | [139] | 2011 | NIR-VIS |
| CVC-13: Multimodal Stereo Dataset (1) | [140] | 2012 | LWIR-VIS |
| CVC-15: Multimodal Stereo Dataset (2) | [141] | 2013 | LWIR-VIS |
| Pedestrian Inf./Visible Stereo Video Dataset | [142] | 2014 | LWIR-VIS |
| Maritime Imagery in the VIS and IR Spectrums (VAIS) | [143] | 2015 | VIS, LWIR |
| RGB/NIR Dehazing Data Set | [144] | 2017 | NIR-VIS |
| KAIST Multi-Spectral Day/Night Data Set | [145] | 2018 | LWIR-VIS-Stereo 3D Lidar-GPS/IMU |
| RGB-T Object Tracking (RGBT234) | [146] | 2019 | LWIR-VIS |
| CASIA-SURF Anti-Spoofing Dataset | [147] | 2019 | NIR-VIS Depth |
| FLIR Thermal Dataset for Algorithm Training | [FLIR-REF] | 2019 | LWIR-VIS |
| Tufts Face Database | [148] | 2020 | NIR-LWIR-VIS Facial Sketch-3D |
| EDGE20 Dataset | [149] | 2020 | NIR-VIS |
| Freiburg Thermal Dataset | [150] | 2020 | LWIR-VIS |

geometric distortions due to different camera's lens, perspective projections, and stereo effects. Due to all the challenges mentioned above, image registration approaches based on keypoint detection [151], usually fail mainly due to the different appearance of the same image content.

Early approaches on cross- and multi-spectral registration based on local feature detection and matching focus on adapting gradient-based descriptors to work between $[0, \pi]$ instead of $[0, 2\pi]$ to reduce the effect of changes in the gradient direction between images from two different spectral bands. This simple yet effective strategy was used in [152] to modify a SIFT descriptor to match VIS-NIR images. A similar strategy was considered in [22], but in this case to adapt a HOG descriptor to be used in the VIS and thermal IR scenario. Trying to adapt already existing feature descriptors, [153] proposes a local patch similarity function to find correspondences between VIS and LWIR images. The proposed solution consists of a combination

Figure 3.2: Cross-spectral image registration: VIS image (left), LWIR image (center), result from image registration and fusion through a Discrete Wavelet Transform (DWT) (top right), and result from image registration and fusion by means of a monochrome threshold (bottom right). The example images are taken from [136].

of a tuned version of Difference of Gaussians (DoG) detector [154] and a local Edge Histogram Descriptor (EHD) [155]. Figure 3.2 shows fused images obtained after registering VIS-LWIR pairs in [153]. Although interesting results are obtained in these illustrations, the main issue with this *hand-crafted* cross-spectral feature descriptors based image registration lies on the rather low number of correspondences compared to VIS-VIS image pairs. However, with a large number of found correspondences, a more robust and accurate image registration result is obtained.

Having in mind the aforementioned limitation and trying to increase the number of correspondences, some novel approaches were proposed and specifically designed for cross-spectral image registration. These approaches are based on the observation that there usually is a strong correlation between object boundaries at the different spectra. In other words, texture information is lost while object boundary information remains similar and well visible in both spectra [156–158]. This observation was also considered in [159], where the authors propose a new feature descriptor to match information from different spectral bands such as VIS-NIR or VIS-LWIR. The proposed approach describes the neighborhood of feature points combining frequency and spatial information in a multi-scale and multi-oriented Log-Gabor filter.

In recent years, different deep learning-based neural network architectures were proposed in the literature to find correspondences between features of images obtained from different spectral bands. These correspondences are then used as reference to register the given cross-spectral images. Such DCNN-based architectures are trained to measure similarity between

ROIs obtained from the given cross-spectral images. In this context, three different DCNN architectures to measure the similarity of cross-spectral image patches (VIS-NIR and VIS-LWIR) are evaluated in [17]. The evaluated architectures are chosen as follows. (1) Two-channel network: this architecture is fed by an input image patch of two channels, where each channel corresponds to one of the two patches to be compared (one from each spectral band). The network consists of a series of convolutions, ReLU and max-pooling layers, and a final linear layer that works as the metric network. (2) Siamese network: this architecture consists of two individual DCNN feature extractor networks with shared parameters that process each patch (one from each spectral band) independently and a final metric network that represents a distance metric. (3) Pseudo-Siamese network: this architecture is a Siamese network but without sharing parameters, i.e., each feature network is different from the other. In the study, the authors also compare these three architectures with the *hand-crafted* cross-spectral feature descriptors mentioned above. Experimental results show that in all the cases, the DCNN-based approaches outperform adaptations from classical feature descriptors in terms of matching performance. Additionally, the study also shows that some DCNN architectures are capable of generalizing between different cross-spectral domains. The only negative point with the DCNN-based approaches lies on the speed: the evaluated networks are much slower than classical solutions. An extension to the above-mentioned Siamese DCNN architectures was presented in [160]. The approach is referred to as quadruplets and was inspired by the triplet network proposed in [161], but adapted to be used with cross-spectral image pairs. The proposed quadruplets structure needs as input two pairs of matched samples, hence at the training stage it receives matching samples, which are the two given patches ($VIS_1$,$LWIR_1$) and ($VIS_2$,$LWIR_2$), and non-matching samples, which are the combinations of the given patches ($VIS_1$,$LWIR_2$) and ($VIS_2$,$LWIR_1$). As a result, it requires less training data.

In contrast to the DCNN-based approaches presented above, where the similarity between features extracted from each spectral band is evaluated at the end of the architecture, a novel DCNN architecture is presented in [162]: the Aggregated Feature Difference learning Network (AFD-Net). It uses feature differences at the different levels of the architecture to find matches across spectral bands such as VIS-NIR. The proposed architecture makes use of a domain invariant feature extraction network that is based on instance normalization. More recently, a deep self-correlation descriptor was presented in [163] for establishing dense correspondences between cross-spectral images. Like in the previous method, the proposed DCNN architecture also computes the feature correlation at different levels of the network using a pyramidal structure. The proposed approach shows a great robustness to non-rigid image deformations and different modality variations.

Although cross-spectral image registration has been largely studied considering different sources and distortions, it still remain as an open problem with different challenging scenarios to be tackles especially when registering VIS and thermal IR images. A great number of solutions have been proposed in the remote sensing and medical imaging communities. In spite of that, the problem still deserves to be revisited in particular by using novel deep learning based approaches. Furthermore, new applications related to new hardware on the market such as mobile devices, surveillance, or driver assistance open promising opportunities to be explored.

## 3.2    IMAGE COLORIZATION

Image colorization is an essential image processing task that has been largely studied in recent years in the context of the VIS spectrum to automatically colorize black and white photos or classic movies for instance [164]. It is a very challenging problem as it is severely ill-posed since two out of the three image channels are lost. Although the semantic information of the scene may be helpful in some cases (e.g., the sky is blue, grass is usually green, clouds are usually white) it is not the case when the scene contains human made objects such as a table, a car, or a house that can severely vary in terms of color or texture. Please refer to Fig. 1.5 in Chapter 1 for a highly meaningful example. Furthermore, the colorization problem is also affected by changes in illumination, variation in viewpoints, shadows in the scene, and occlusions.

Several methods have been proposed to solve this challenging task [165, 166]. It is obvious that machine and deep learning-based methods are a suitable and popular approach [167, 168]. The proposed methods mostly differ in the way they obtain and treat the data for modeling the correspondences between gray-scale and color. Coarsely speaking, colorization techniques can be classified into parametric and nonparametric approaches. Parametric methods learn prediction functions from large datasets of color images at training time, posing the problem as either regression onto continuous color space or classification of quantified color values. On the other hand, nonparametric methods utilize an input gray-scale image and firstly define one or more color reference images (provided by a user or automatically retrieved) as source data. Then, following the image analogy framework, color is transferred onto the input image from analogous regions of the reference image(s).

The aforementioned classification is based on the visible spectrum image colorization approaches. IR image colorization somehow shares common properties and problems with these monochromatic image colorization approaches. There are different motivations to colorize IR images: if an operator has to analyze and evaluate the scene content of a NIR image, a visual representation he is familiar with may help him to fulfill his task. This can be an RGB image that results from NIR colorization. In the case of thermal IR images, sometimes it is required to colorize them in order to use approaches already developed for the visible spectrum (e.g., pedestrian detection [169]). Finally, other approaches that could be also included in this section are those tackling the generation of IR images from the corresponding RGB ones. These approaches are intended to handle the lack of training data and annotations in the IR imagery in comparison with the VIS spectrum domain. For instance, in [170] it is proposed to transform labeled RGB videos intro thermal IR videos in order to use the corresponding annotations for training a DCNN architecture for the task of object tracking in thermal IR videos.

IR image colorization was approached as a gray-scale colorization task in the literature utilizing deep learning techniques. In [171], a multi-scale DCNN was proposed together with classical computer vision post-processing techniques to perform an estimation of RGB values for a given NIR image. In [172], two fully automatic transformation methods of thermal IR images to VIS color images were presented. The authors propose a more sophisticated objective function in order to tackle misalignment issues between the two visible and thermal modalities. The methods were evaluated with publicly available datasets (urban driving scenarios) showing perceptually realistic results. In [173], a novel approach for colorizing NIR images was presented. It uses an encoder-decoder DCNN architecture followed by a secondary assistant network. The assistant network is a shallow encoder-decoder used to enhance the edges and improve the output. Like in the previous case, the proposed approach is evaluated in urban driving scenarios.

In contrast to the just discussed approaches, there are several recent publications that heavily rely on generative models to perform image-to-image translation between IR and RGB representations following both supervised and unsupervised schemes. Generative Adversarial Networks (GANs) introduced in [174] are probably the most significant recent improvements in the field of generative models and they are extensively used for image-to-image translation [175]. In [176], one of the first NIR image colorization approaches based on the usage of a GAN architecture was presented. A triplet DCNN model is proposed: each channel is trained independently in a supervised scheme using pairs of NIR-VIS images. Another GAN based approach is considered in [177], but in this case to colorize thermal IR images. The authors propose a conditional GAN to generate RGB images. The architecture is trained using a coarse-to-fine generator and a composite objective function that combines: content, adversarial, perceptual, and Total Variation (TV) losses to generate realistic results. Previous approaches are suitable when paired and aligned images are provided for the training process. In the case of unpaired images, the task can be tackled by a GAN architecture in the unsupervised context under a cyclic structure (CycleGAN [178]). CycleGANs learn to map images from one domain (source domain) onto another domain (target domain). They are particularly useful if paired images are not available. Cross-domain images used for training do not even have to show the same scene. Such a CycleGAN architecture for colorizing unpaired NIR-RGB images was introduced for instance in [179]. Figure 3.3 shows some results obtained with the unsupervised approach presented in [179].

As mentioned above, the IR image colorization problem can be considered in both NIR and LWIR spectral bands. In both cases, supervised and unsupervised approaches were proposed in the literature. It should be noticed that supervised approaches heavily rely on the pixel-wise registered data used during the training process. In general, in the case of NIR image colorization the RGB-NIR Scene Dataset [139] is used as a reference for training and evaluating results. On the other hand, in the LWIR image colorization case, the KAIST Multi-Spectral Day/Night Data Set [145] is considered that should not be confused with the KAIST Multispectral Pedestrian Benchmark [63]. In both cases a quantitative evaluation is obtained by

| NIR | Colorized NIR [179] | Ground Truth |

Figure 3.3: Images from the CycleGAN based approach presented in [179]: NIR input image (left), result from [179] (center), and ground truth RGB image (right).

measuring at every pixel the angular error between the obtained RGB and the corresponding ground truth value. Angular error is chosen since this measure is quite similar to the human visual perception systems. There are studies that show the high correlation between the angular error and the perception of a human observer [180].

## 3.3    ENHANCEMENT TECHNIQUES

The cross-spectral approach has been also largely used as a way to exploit advantages from one domain toward the enhancement of images in the other domain. Cross-spectral image enhancement can be considered in both directions from IR domain to VIS spectrum by improving haze removal in the VIS spectrum using IR images for instance as well as from VIS spectrum to IR domain by performing guided IR super resolution or thermal IR image filtering for example. In this section, some of the different possibilities are reviewed summarizing the main ideas behind each one of these *collaborative* schemes.

**Guided Super Resolution:** As mentioned in Section 2.3, different images super resolution techniques were presented during the last decades. Although most of them are intended for the VIS spectrum, in recent years some adaptations or novel approaches were proposed for the thermal IR image domain. In spite of these contributions, the difference between resolution of VIS spectrum and IR images, in particular thermal IR images, is still considerable due to the nature and the market of the sensors. This large difference in resolution motivated the research community, when working on cross-spectral computer vision, to develop strategies that allow to take advantage of high resolution (HR) VIS spectrum images to generate super resolution thermal IR images. These contributions can be considered as a kind of *guided approaches*. Some of them are reviewed in the remainder of this section. In [181], one of the first schemes was presented to guide super resolution for thermal IR images by a HR color image. The IR super resolution guidance is based on the fact that discontinuities in the IR image often co-occur with color or brightness changes in the corresponding color image. A cost function can be defined to find the sub-pixel values in the IR image. The authors propose a prototype of an IR-color multi-sensor imaging system that allows for collecting images and videos from different scenes to evaluate the proposed approach. In contrast to this approach, other authors [182–184] propose novel deep learning-based guided super-resolution methods. In [182], it was proposed to mitigate the relatively low resolution of thermal IR cameras with respect to RGB cameras by using a Thermal Image Enhancement (TEN) DCNN. The neural network is trained in a end-to-end scheme so that it learns to map a given single low-resolution image to the desired high-resolution image. The proposed lightweight TEN network has two main components: the first module is responsible for extracting feature maps while the second module produces the final high-quality image. In [184], the thermal IR super-resolution images are obtained through a visual-thermal fusion model that integrates high-frequency information from the VIS spectrum domain. A GAN is proposed to fuse features from the VIS spectrum together with features of the thermal IR image.

Figure 3.4: Images from a RGB/NIR dataset [144] intended for dehazing algorithms' evaluation: RGB image affected by haze (left), related NIR image affected by haze (center), and related ground truth RGB image (right).

In [183], high-frequency features (i.e., edge maps) are extracted in a pyramidal way from the VIS image. These features are integrated into the super resolution thermal IR image by means of an attention based fusion network. The extraction and integration of multi-level edges allows the super resolution network to process textures-to-object level information progressively, enabling more straightforward identification of overlapping edges between input images.

**RGB Image Dehazing:** Color image dehazing is another image processing task that can benefit from cross-spectral information, in particular from those spectral bands less affected by haze related atmospheric phenomena such as the NIR spectral band. Figure 3.4 shows a hazy RGB and NIR image pair together with the corresponding ground truth that can be used for evaluating cross- or multi-spectral dehazing algorithms. Different cross-spectral dehazing techniques were proposed in the literature, which differ from each other in the way information is fused. For instance, Schaul et al. [21] propose fusing NIR and VIS images of the same scene to produce a dehazed color image. The proposed method transforms the given RGB image into a luminance-chrominance color space. The extracted luminance of the VIS image is fused with the corresponding NIR representation. The result is considered as the new luminance representation that is recombined with the original chrominance information. This fusion is performed in a multi-resolution way using an edge-preserving filtering to minimize artifacts. A NIR and VIS image fusion scheme is presented in [185] to dehaze color images: the weighted fusion is based on a haze distribution model that considers the difference of infrared and blue light intensity together with dark channel prior information. Then, according to the haze distribution map, NIR and VIS light information is fused and the final representation enhanced through a set of filtering stages. The proposed method is simple but efficient and achieves high fidelity and real-time performance. The weighting of NIR images using a transmission map is also used in [186] to fuse NIR and VIS spectrum images. The authors propose to restore the image contrast by fusing detail components of the NIR image into the VIS image. In contrast to the previous approaches, depth information can be a valuable source of additional information. In [187], a dehazing mechanism is proposed based on the depth map and airlight color estimation together with the NIR-VIS spectrum scene statistics. All this information is used to form a haze-free

image. Depth information is also considered in [188], where a new NIR fusion model is proposed by combined the proposed new color and depth based regularization with the conventional haze degradation model. The color regularization estimates color information for the unknown haze-free color image, while the depth regularization allows the estimated depth maps not to be largely deviated, it also transfers the details and natural-looking colors of the colorized NIR image into the initial dehazed image.

In order to evaluate the performance of different approaches, realistic datasets are needed. These datasets should include both RGB and NIR images captured from the same scene at the same time. Actually, images should be correctly registered and aligned in order to use IR information at the pixel level for the dehazing process. The dataset should also include ground truth from the provided RGB/NIR hazy image pairs. Due to the challenging requirements, there are not that many datasets available fulfilling these properties. One of the few cross-spectral datasets that includes RGB and NIR images synchronously captured and correctly registered is presented in [144]. The dataset also includes ground truth dehazed images to be used as a reference during performance evaluation of different algorithms. In order to fulfill the requirements mentioned above, in some datasets hazy images are generated synthetically. The main issue with such datasets lies on the fact that synthetic haze does not show typical sensor characteristics such as sensor noise. Furthermore, it is just a mathematical model that depends on the wavelength of the light and the size of atmospheric particles. We can use such fully or partially synthetic data to evaluate dehazing methods in various scenarios, where the acquisition of real data is difficult or expensive. But it is obvious that the desired performance of the dehazing algorithm under realistic conditions is not guaranteed.

**Others:** In addition to the guided super resolution and RGB image dehazing, cross-spectral approaches are also used in other image enhancement-related tasks such as filtering and edge detection. Some contributions on these topics are summarized next. Regarding cross-spectral filtering strategies, Shibata et al. [189] propose filtering IR images using information from the corresponding color image. The authors use a novel misalignment-robust joint filter based on weight-volume based image composition and joint-filter cost volume. The proposed approach starts first by translating the original guidance image. Then, a cross-modal cost volume, widely used in stereo vision for estimating disparity maps, is used to compute a weight volume representation. Finally, this weight-volume based representation, which takes into account both images, is used to generate the filtered images by minimizing the cost pixel-by-pixel. Experimental results in different cross-spectral representations show the robustness of the proposed approach. In order to filter noisy VIS images, Zhuo et al. [190] utilize a hybrid camera system to simultaneously record VIS and NIR images. Both cameras are optically aligned with the same focal length and aperture to guarantee geometric alignment of each pair. A NIR flash is used to take sharp noise-free NIR images. The VIS image is denoised and its details are enhanced using its corresponding NIR flash image. In [191], the authors follow a similar idea of using well-illuminated NIR images to denoise RGB images. They adapt the Block-matching and 3D filtering (BM3D) algorithm [192] to handle and utilize multi-spectral RGB-NIR image pairs. In addition to the filtering approaches, the edge detection task was also tackled under such a kind of cross-spectral domains. In [193], a DCNN architecture called Multi-Spectral Image Holistically-Nested Edge Detection (MSI-HED) was proposed to extract edges of the structures in the given RGB image by using both the RGB and corresponding NIR image. In this work, a single-sensor RGB+NIR camera is considered, hence a pixel accurate registration is guaranteed. The presented approach consists of an adaptation of the Holistically-Nested Edge Detection (HED) approach [194] that was proposed before to extract edges from RGB images. Although HED and MSI-HED result in similar quantitative results, qualitatively MSI-HED gives better results. In other words, NIR information can help to better detect edges, in particular small details. It should be noticed that MSI-HED was trained just with edges annotated in the VIS spectrum image. Even the task of deblurring can benefit from a cross- or multi-spectral approach utilizing aligned RGB-NIR image pairs [195].

All the approaches presented in this section are developed assuming a correctly registered set of cross-spectral image pairs is available. This means that those approaches may be affected by misalignment. The development of robust approaches able to perform cross-spectral image enhancement from coarsely registered cross-spectral images is still an open problem and there is an opportunity to tackle such a challenging task.

C H A P T E R   4

# Detection, Classification, and Tracking

Automatic image and video exploitation or content analysis is a technique to extract higher-level information from a scene such as objects, behavior, (inter-)actions, environment, or even weather conditions. The relevant information is assumed to be contained in the two-dimensional signal provided in an image (width and height in pixels) or the three-dimensional signal provided in a video (width, height, and time). But also intermediate-level information such as object classes [196], locations [197], or motion [198] can help applications to fulfill certain tasks such as intelligent compression [199], video summarization [200], or video retrieval [201]. Usually, videos with their temporal dimension are a richer source of data compared to single images [202] and thus certain video content can be extracted from videos only such as object motion or object behavior. Often, machine learning or nowadays deep learning techniques are utilized to model prior knowledge about object or scene appearance using labeled training samples [203, 204]. After a *learning* phase, these models are then applied in real world applications, which is called *inference*.

With this focus on image and video exploitation, we aim at analyzing methods and algorithms that can be used with IR cameras for the automation of processes needed for industrial robots [205], self-driving vehicles [206, 207], or automated surveillance at the edge [208].

## 4.1    CHANGE DETECTION

From a historical perspective, the task of change detection is among the first that was tackled utilizing thermal IR video data. For surveillance and reconnaissance applications as well as for search and rescue, long-range cameras are used for the observation of objects at a great distance of up to many kilometers. The detection and analysis of such objects can be well supported with any kind of salience. This salience can originate from object motion but still the task is highly challenging due to low object resolution or atmospheric perturbations such as turbulence (see Section 2.2). An additional source of salience though can be the thermal IR object signature. Humans or man-made objects are usually observed in the mentioned applications. We can expect that often their temperature is warmer than the surrounding environment and thus their radiation is stronger. Hence, the combination of object motion and visual salience based on the thermal IR signature greatly simplifies the task of motion or change detection.

More specific, changes in videos can be an object moving within a mostly static scene as well as objects that appear or disappear in between two images that show the same scene with a certain time gap in between. This time gap is application dependent and actually can vary between seconds or even milliseconds (short-term change detection) and years (long-term change detection). Since short-term changes usually originate from movement currently taking place, it is also known as motion segmentation. The detection of such changes is an important step to reach a higher level of automation in various computer vision-related applications such as visual surveillance, search and rescue, or robotics. An operator staring at a monitor with multiple surveillance videos displayed in parallel can easily miss relevant events. Instead, automatic change detection can be used to raise an alarm and thus catch the attention of the operator only in case of noteworthy events such as motion in a restricted area or unaccompanied luggage in a public place. Autonomous vehicles or mobile robots should be aware of any changes in their environment to avoid collisions or to interact properly. In [209], the authors state that change detection can be an important pre-processing step in many applications, in which object detection, tracking, or classification shall be limited to moving objects only. The key challenge arises from the necessity to distinguish between relevant and irrelevant changes in images: while moving objects such as vehicles or persons as well as appearing objects within a time gap such as luggage or buildings usually are relevant changes, there are many irrelevant changes like camera noise, different weather conditions such as rain or moving clouds, properties of the environment such as falling leaves or movement of waves, global illumination changes due to clouds passing by the sun or switching on the room lights, local illumination changes due to shadows or light spots, or local motion due to atmospheric perturbations such as turbulence. Figure 4.1 shows a scene affected by turbulence with several small-scaled objects in the image due to the large distance between the camera and the scene. It is obvious that detecting such objects is challenging especially when sensing the scene is affected by atmospheric turbulence. Furthermore, for a moving camera, the entire scene seems to move, so image registration and alignment is necessary to determine the stationary scene background and thus compensate for camera motion. The mentioned challenges are the same for both the VIS and all IR spectral bands.

Since change detection is a rather special topic in computer vision often related to security applications, not many public datasets exist in the literature. There is only one benchmark specifically dedicated to change detection that not only provides VIS but also thermal IR images: the changedetection.net (CDnet 2014) benchmark presented in [210]. It consists of 53 videos subdivided in eleven categories such as challenging weather, dynamic background, low frame rate, or shadows. The duration of each video is between 900 and 7,000 frames and there are more than 160,000 frames in total. Among the aforementioned categories are two highly relevant: the *thermal* category with 21,100 frames in five LWIR sequences and *air turbulence* with 15,700 frames in 4 NIR videos. Each image sequence contains at least one foreground object. Ground truth is provided for each single image of the sequence by foreground masks, in which each pixel is labeled as either foreground or background. This indicates that we have

Figure 4.1: Example images taken from the CDnet 2014 dataset [210] showing moving objects in a long-range distance (left) together with their related ground truth (right) for change detection. The red arrows indicate the moving objects in the original image.

an image segmentation problem here, where the goal is to separate individual foreground and background pixels and to cluster foreground pixels to connected components [211]. Further reading about image segmentation in general is provided in [212] and [213]. Following [210], the quantitative evaluation can be done using measures such as false positive rate, false negative rate, precision, recall, and f-score that will be discussed in Section 4.2 already. The important difference, however, is that these measures are applied pixel-wise here, while they are applied to bounding boxes in object detection benchmarks. In addition to the CDnet 2014 benchmark, nearly each of the object detection and multiple object tracking datasets that will be discussed in the next sections of this chapter can be used to develop and evaluate change detection algorithms. The reason is that most objects in these datasets are moving. However, the ground truth is provided as bounding boxes only and hence the quantitative evaluation cannot be performed pixel-wise.

In Fig. 4.2, an example pipeline for change detection is visualized. This pipeline is similar for both VIS and IR images. If the camera is moving, the first step is image registration. We assume to have a background model that is represented by a background image. This background image contains the stationary scene background only. In order to compensate for the camera motion, the background image is aligned to the current image. First, keypoints need to be detected. Keypoints are local image features such as prominent corners or points within the image that can be re-identified even across different camera perspectives. Kanade-Lucas-Tomasi (KLT) feature tracking [214] is still a popular method for keypoint detection, but also Scale Invariant Features Transform (SIFT) [154] features, or Speeded Up Robust Features (SURF) [215] are commonly used. A robust set of point correspondences between the current and the background image is found by keypoint matching and can be used to estimate a homography as a global camera motion model according to [216]. 3D parallax effects can disturb image registration but can be handled by local image registration and parallax handling [217, 218]. With this estimated

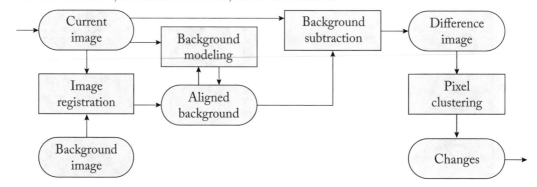

Figure 4.2: Typical processing pipeline for change detection.

camera motion, the background image can be warped to achieve pixel-wise alignment between the current and the background image. A maybe slightly outdated but recommendable survey about image registration is provided in [151].

In order to detect foreground pixels, the stationary scene background needs to be modeled. Usually, there are several assumptions made for approaches that learn the stationary background: (1) consecutive frames in the image sequence strongly overlap and are aligned; (2) each image contains significantly more background than foreground objects; and (3) a sufficient number of frames is available to capture irrelevant changes within the background such as variation in illumination or weather. Traditional approaches use for example pixel-wise Gaussian Mixture Models (GMMs) to learn the expected intensity or color variation of each pixel [219, 220]. This is a probabilistic approach that needs a minimum number of sample images to produce a robust statistical model. Usually, hundreds or even thousands of images are necessary to learn such a background model. In case of a moving camera, however, even small image misalignment can severely affect the model quality and less images should be used such as 30 [336]. More recent pixel-wise background learning approaches such as Visual Background Extractor (ViBe) [221] are able to achieve higher robustness against variations within the scene background and to create more robust models faster. In case of fast-moving cameras mounted on airborne platforms or cameras with a low frame rate, short-term background learning using ten or less images can be and option [222, 223]. Recommended literature about background modeling is provided in [224] and [225]. An alternative to background modeling and subtraction is frame-differencing [226] that does not need a background model but just few (usually 1–2) reference frames. Two- or three-frame differencing approaches are common. A survey on frame differencing approaches for airborne applications is provided by Sommer et al. [223]. Another option is performing optical flow [227] to detect motion independent of the camera motion. Dense optical flow, however, strongly uses smoothing and regularization to make the flow vector field become dense. This can be a drawback when detecting small-scaled, slowly moving objects in the image: their motion can disappear when calculating dense optical flow.

By subtracting the background image pixel-wise from the current image or by applying frame differencing, the so-called difference image is calculated. Parts of the scene that do not belong to the learned stationary background are expected to produce pixels of bright intensity values within the difference image. These pixels can be clustered in order to represent changes by connected and highlighted image regions. But not only relevant changes such as moving objects appear but also noise and clutter due to camera noise, image misalignment, illumination changes, or environmental conditions. Hence, pixel clustering usually follows pre-processing methods such as morphological operations as well as intensity thresholding to produce a binary image with 0s for background and 1s for foreground. Finally, connected image regions with a pixel area smaller than a certain threshold are rejected. Most of the change detection approaches presented in this section are originally proposed and developed for VIS images only. However, they can be transferred and applied directly to the IR spectral bands as several authors show [260, 277, 278]. But no author is discussing the specific properties and differences of IR change detection.

The entire process of background subtraction or frame differencing can be learned end-to-end by DCNNs as already demonstrated by multiple authors [228–230]. Just recently proposed approaches [231–233] show that these DCNNs can be made agnostic to the used spectrum as they perform well on the CDnet 2014 dataset that contains both VIS and IR sequences. However, there are several important aspects to consider: DCNNs for change detection can be scene dependent, i.e., they can only be applied to the scene they were trained with, or scene independent [234]. For a higher generalization ability, it is usually desired to be scene independent [233]. 3D convolutions are a powerful tool to capture both appearance and motion information simultaneously [235]. However, they can significantly increase the number of trainable parameters in the DCNN and hence they can extend both training and inference time. Potential camera motion is often not considered, which again lowers the approach's generalization ability. Finally, it can be proven that appearance information in addition to the motion cues is beneficial to distinguish between relevant and irrelevant motion. Semantic segmentation is a promising approach to represent appearance for change detection [236, 237], but the proposed approach then will (1) be highly dependent on the performance of the semantic segmentation method and (2) most likely not be agnostic anymore to the used spectrum.

## 4.2    OBJECT DETECTION AND CLASSIFICATION

Autonomous systems need to understand how to detect and classify objects of interest. Self-driving vehicles, for example, must be able to detect obstacles potentially blocking or crossing their way in order to prevent collisions. They even need to distinguish between certain object classes like pedestrians or cyclists, who can get physically harmed in case of a collision easily, less threatened objects like other vehicles, or invulnerable objects such as traffic signs or street bollards. Similar demands exist for industrial robots that interact with humans or various systems for surveillance or search and rescue. In addition, there are many more applications in navigation [238], intelligent shopping [239], social media [240], or smart mobile devices [241], in which object detection and classification play a key role. Different kinds of sensors can be used to perceive the environment that surrounds an autonomous system. Among the most prominent ones are lidar, radar, ultrasonic, camera, or various sensor combinations. The two main benefits of using cameras is that they can sense purely passive, if there is no need for active illumination, and that they can capture the appearance of the scene and the present objects. In fact, the appearance is probably the most important source of information for visual object detection and classification [242] as we do not consider any additional information here such as context knowledge or depth, which is usually acquired by stereo cameras, time-of-flight cameras, or structure from motion.

As it was already mentioned earlier that each spectral band has its own specific properties, it is strongly dependent on the application, which spectrum may be the best for solving a certain detection or classification problem. The NIR spectrum for example usually needs scene illumination but it is less affected by natural illumination effects such as shadows or sun reflections. In [243], for example, it is discussed that NIR thus fits well to be applied for an automotive night vision system. On the contrary, surveillance and military applications often require passive sensing to minimize the risk of getting exposed. The thermal MWIR and LWIR bands are appropriate therefore as mentioned in [7]. Furthermore, LWIR cameras can provide better imagery for human detection especially in complex outdoor scenarios with masking background texture or lack of illumination. Several authors demonstrated that in such scenarios the thermal signature of persons is more prominent compared to the VIS signature [63, 244, 245]. In [244], it is also shown that in scenes with a similar temperature of environment and objects like on streets during summer, vehicles can be detected more reliably in the VIS instead of the LWIR spectrum.

Before discussing the available public datasets, it should be clarified how we define the problems of object detection and object classification and how they can be quantitatively evaluated. In object classification, the goal is to determine all the classes that appear in an image. Hence, we want to answer the question *What can we see in this image?* These classes can then be attached to the image as meta data such as tags or labels to explain the image content. It is not unusual that the objects are already cropped and centered within the image. The challenge here is not to determine the exact number of objects or the object locations within the image but to distinguish between hundreds or even thousands of different classes. Example datasets and benchmarks are the ImageNet Large-Scale Visual Recognition Challenge (ILSVRC) [246] or Pascal Visual Object Classification (VOC) [247]. These datasets do not only come with many samples images for the present classes but also with so-called ground truth annotations that tell us the humanly sensed classification result and hence can be used for development and evaluation. The quantitative evaluation for challenges with more than two classes can be done using the mean Average Precision (mAP) and multi-class confusion matrices. For already cropped images that contain only one or no object and a two-class problem consisting of object and non-object samples, we can consider correct classifications of objects as True Positives (TP) and correct

Figure 4.3: Example images taken from the FLIR Thermal Dataset including detected objects indicated by bounding boxes with related class labels (source: FLIR).

classifications of non-objects as True Negatives (TN). Incorrect classifications are then called either False Negatives (FN) for objects or False Positives (FP) for non-objects. When varying the classifier confidence threshold during evaluation, a Receiver Operating Characteristic (ROC) curve can be created that plots the true positive rate against the false positive rate. The Area Under the Curve (AUC) can be calculated to represent a classifiers potential with one single value only. There is quite some recommendable literature available for further reading about this topic [248–250]. In object detection, the challenge is not only to determine the presence of certain objects inside an image but also to detect all instances and locate them. Hence, we answer the questions *How many objects of a certain class does the image contain?* (= instances) and *Where are they located inside the image?*. For an image that contains three persons, a correct classification result would be to assign the label *person* or *persons* to the image. A correct detection result, however, would be to highlight each instance of a desired object class with a bounding box and a class label. Prominent examples for detection datasets and benchmarks are Common Objects in Context (COCO) [251] for multi-class object detection and the Caltech Pedestrian Detection Benchmark [252] for two-class object detection: person vs. background. Example images taken from the FLIR Thermal Dataset,[1] which is currently one of the most popular public thermal IR datasets for object detection, are shown in Fig. 4.3. The ground truth annotations are given by bounding boxes that surround each object instance. The already-mentioned evaluation metric

[1]https://www.flir.com/oem/adas/adas-dataset-form/ (last accessed: April 2, 2021).

mAP can be used here, too. But as the object location is a crucial aspect of object detection, we first need to discuss what conditions must be satisfied so that an object can be considered TP. Since each detection is represented by a bounding box, the Intersection over Union (IoU) criterion can be used to calculate the overlap between a detection and a ground truth box. An IoU threshold of 0.5 is a recommended default value [247], i.e., a detection is considered TP, if it overlaps with a related ground truth box at least halfway, and FP otherwise. However, TN is not a meaningful measure in detection since images are screened for usually only few objects of interest and hence nearly all samples will be TN. So, instead of using true positive rate, false positive rate, and ROC curves, we can use precision, recall, and precision-recall curves that consider TP, FP, and FN, but not TN. Another popular measure is the f-score, which is the harmonic mean of precision and recall. For pedestrian detection, however, it is common to plot the False Positives Per Image (FPPI) against the false negative rate (= miss rate). Further reading is provided in [249] or [252].

An overview of the currently available public datasets for object detection and classification in IR images is given in Table 4.1. Besides the name of the dataset and the related publication together with the year, we also mention the spectral bands that are used and the number of object classes within each dataset. If ground truth annotations are provided, the number of labels is written in the table as well. The OSU Thermal Pedestrian Database [253] was introduced back in 2005. It consists of 10 LWIR image sequences acquired by a stationary camera and 984 ground truth bounding boxes for present persons. The Terravic Research Infrared Database [254] consists of 23 LWIR image sequences in total and can be used for the detection of persons or weapons. However, no ground truth bounding boxes are provided. In [255], the CSIR-CSIO Moving Object Thermal Infrared Imagery Dataset (MOTIID) was presented. There are 18 LWIR sequences containing 5 classes of different moving objects such as persons, animals, and vehicles. No ground truth annotations are given. The CVC FIR Datasets [14] for person detection come with 15,058 ground truth boxes. Additionally, VIS and synthetic videos are contained but not aligned to the IR videos. The LSI FIR Datasets [13] are subdivided in two sets for person classification and detection. The classification subset contains cropped samples of size $32 \times 64$ pixels each with 16,202 pedestrians and 65,440 non-pedestrians in total. The detection subset consists of 15,224 fourteen-bit single images with annotated pedestrians. The ETH Thermal Infrared Dataset [256] consists of eight image sequences showing humans and animals. Ground truth annotations are given for both detection and tracking. The FLIR Thermal Dataset for Algorithm Training[2] provides 10,228 annotated object instances of the 5 different classes person, car, bicycle, dog, or other vehicle. It comes with 14-bit and 8-bit image pairs. In addition, related but unaligned and not annotated RGB images are given. The OSU Color-Thermal Database [138] comes with six videos that show two different scenes. It is a multi-spectral dataset with aligned VIS and LWIR bands and can be used for person detection and tracking. Just recently, annotations for person detection were published in [259]. This

---

[2]https://www.flir.com/oem/adas/adas-dataset-form/ (last accessed: April 2, 2021).

Table 4.1: Available public datasets for IR object detection and classification

| Dataset | Related Publication | Year | Spectral Bands | Classes (Labels) |
|---|---|---|---|---|
| OSU Thermal Pedestrian Database | [253] | 2005 | LWIR | 1 (984) |
| Terravic Research Infrared Database | [254] | 2006 | LWIR | 2 (0) |
| CSIR-CSIO Moving Object Thermal Infrared Imagery Dataset (MOTIID) | [255] | 2013 | LWIR | 5 (0) |
| CVC FIR Datasets | [14] | 2013 | LWIR | 1 (15,058) |
| LSI Far Infrared Pedestrian Dataset | [13] | 2013 | LWIR | 1 (16,202) |
| ETH Thermal Infrared Dataset | [256] | 2014 | LWIR | 3 (n/a) |
| FLIR ADAS Thermal Dataset | – | 2019 | LWIR | 5 (10,228) |
| OSU Color-Thermal Database | [138] | 2007 | VIS, LWIR | 1 (0) |
| KAIST Multispectral Pedestrian Detection | [63] | 2015 | VIS, LWIR | 1 (13,853) |
| Maritime Detection, Classification, and Tracking (MarDCT) | [257] | 2015 | VIS, LWIR | 5 (n/a) |
| Maritime Imagery in the VIS and IR Spectrums (VAIS) | [143] | 2015 | VIS, LWIR | 6 (1,088) |
| Singapore Maritime Dataset (SMD) | [258] | 2017 | VIS, NIR | 10 (241,292) |
| Multispectral Object Detection | [15] | 2017 | VIS, NIR, MWIR, LWIR | 5 (5,833) |

is noteworthy since the original dataset does not provide any ground truth. However, baseline tracking results can be requested from [260]. The KAIST Multispectral Pedestrian Detection Benchmark [63] can be used for person detection in aligned VIS and LWIR images. Twelve image sequences including bounding boxes for all appearing persons are provided. In contrast to most of the aforementioned datasets, the camera is not stationary but moving, which adds a new challenge for video content analysis here. While the other datasets are relevant mostly for surveillance scenarios, this dataset together with the CVC FIR Datasets is particularly interesting for automotive applications. Multiple authors provide multi-spectral maritime datasets for vessel detection, classification, and tracking [143, 257, 258]. Ground truth annotation is given and especially the Singapore Maritime Dataset (SMD) impresses with labels for 241,292 individual detections subdivided in ten different object classes. In [15], a multi-spectral dataset was presented for automotive applications that consists of images acquired by four cameras in VIS, NIR, MWIR, and LWIR spectra. Ground truth is provided for five classes such as pedestrian or

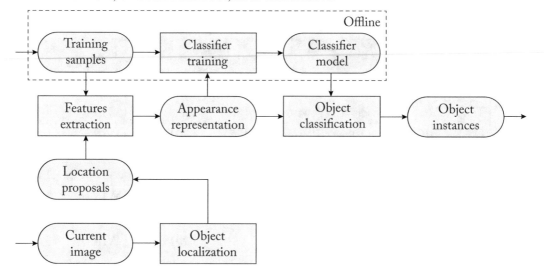

Figure 4.4: Traditional but typical processing pipeline for object detection.

vehicle. Unfortunately, imprecise image registration, out of sync image acquisition times across the spectra, and low image-resolution of $320 \times 240$ pixels for the MWIR sensor diminishes the value of this dataset.

As we can see, most of the presented datasets are tackling the challenge of person detection either exclusively or implicitly. Person detection is a crucial task in automotive and surveillance applications (for more details see Chapter 5) and probably the most popular challenge in object detection. Hence, we will focus on person detection in the remainder of this section. Recalling the aforementioned definition of object detection, we aim at simultaneously solving the localization and the classification problem. Figure 4.4 shows a typical but rather traditional object detection processing pipeline. A training dataset provides positive (person) and negative (background) training samples. Features are extracted from these samples to produce an object appearance representation. These features are used to train a classifier model that is able to distinguish between object and background instances inside the feature space. This training process is run offline. Object localization can be performed using different approaches. The goal is to determine a Region Of Interest (ROI) within the image that potentially contains an object of interest, which is in our case: a person. In [261], a technique was introduced based on exhaustive search called sliding window that was adopted by many authors for object or person detection in the VIS spectrum [262–264]. A search window of certain size is shifted pixel by pixel across the entire image. At each window position, the local image content is analyzed via image classification and the classifier's confidence value is returned. For a highly discriminative classifier, this confidence value should be high for a person within the search window and low for any other image content. If the confidence exceeds a predefined threshold, the detection of a person is accepted. Multiple detections for the same person can be avoided using Non-Maximum Suppression (NMS). Persons at different scales can be detected by resizing the image in between the minimum and maximum expected size of an object. Usually around 50 different scales are considered for person detection according to [265]. Real-time processing capabilities can be met using appropriate approximations and search space reduction such as selective search or randomized search [266, 267]. Sliding windows can be applied in the IR spectra in exactly the same way as for the VIS spectrum and many authors actually use them [63, 268–270]. The described sliding window approach facilitates a holistic object representation modeling a person in its entirety. Part-based models can be an alternative. They first detect body parts as a mid-level representation and then connect them using for example Implicit Shape Models (ISM) as proposed by [271] or Deformable Part Models (DPM) introduced by [272]. Limited literature is available for part-based models applied to IR spectra. In [273], Speeded Up Robust Features (SURF) are used for body part detection followed by an ISM for thermal IR images. A good comparison of holistic and DPM based person detection methods is provided in [274]. In their experiments using the CVC FIR Datasets, DPM outperforms the holistic approaches in most test cases. The reason, however, might be that persons in the CVC FIR Datasets are significantly larger than in most other datasets according to [275]. In general, holistic representation can be preferable for small persons within the image since it is difficult to detect even smaller body parts reliably. If any kind of exhaustive search shall be avoided, there are two options. (1) Background subtraction can be used to detect ROIs of motion within an image sequence. The search space for person detection can then be reduced to these ROIs. For stationary surveillance cameras this can be an option if the limitation to only detecting moving persons is acceptable. Background subtraction is widely used [138, 253, 260, 276–278]. (2) Saliency detection using different thresholding techniques can be applied to segment ROIs with accumulations of high intensity pixels that correspond to hot spots. Person detection is then applied within these ROIs. Such methods are widely used as well [243, 279, 280], but persons necessarily need to be warmer than the surrounding background, which can be a strong limitation. As a conclusion, critical assumptions are made for both options that can be violated regularly and thus can cause overlooked persons leading to FN detections.

In order to solve the object classification problem, features are extracted from the ROIs and image classification methods are used. The extraction of features aims at describing the appearance of an object such as color, shape, or texture. Then, the pre-trained classifier uses those descriptors to model human appearance and apply this model after learning it to determine whether an image contains a person or not. Strong impact was achieved with the well-known Haar-like features evaluated by a Boosted Decision Trees (BDT) classifier and the Histogram of Oriented Gradients (HOG) features exploited by a linear Support Vector Machine (SVM) [262, 263]. In both approaches, the shape of the human silhouette is modeled. Due to absence of color and weakly apparent textures in IR images, edges and shape features particularly play an important role for IR person detection as stated in [279]. In fact, the human silhouette remains observable within the different IR spectra: similar Haar-like or HOG features are produced by a person in bright clothes in front of a dark background in the VIS spectrum and a warm person in front of a cold background in the LWIR spectrum. Analogously, similar features appear for a person in dark clothes in front of a bright background and a person that is colder than its surrounding background like on a hot day in a dessert for example. Hence, the application of Haar-like features with BDT and HOGs with SVM became very popular for person detection in both the NIR band [281–283] and the thermal IR bands [244, 253, 268, 270, 284]. In the meantime, channel features were introduced in the VIS spectrum as a generalization of Haar-like features in [264] and then steadily improved [266]. In combination with a BDT classifier, channel features used to be state-of-the-art for several years. As they are directly applicable to IR images as well, several authors used them for person detection in the VIS/LWIR multi-spectral KAIST dataset (see Table 4.1) [63, 275] or in the thermal IR spectra [285, 286]. Different other approaches for IR person classification were considered in recent literature: Local Binary Patterns (LBP) can be used to describe texture and are analyzed in [274] for their potential to complement HOG features. The detection rate increases for daylight but not for nighttime images. Since the authors are using the multi-spectral VIS/FIR CVC-14 dataset (see Table 4.1), it seems that human specific textures are more apparent during daytime and, thus, LBP can improve detection performance mainly under such conditions. In [279], various descriptor/classifier combinations are evaluated such as LBP, HOG, Integral Channel Features (ChnFtrs), or Discrete Cosine Transform (DCT) features and various classifiers such as Random Forest (RF), BDT, or SVM. The best detection rate is achieved using either DCT features or ChnFtrs. In [287], dense HOGs are proposed that are able to capture signatures of low-resolution IR targets. In a combination with a Bag-of-Words (BoW) approach used to create a sparse representation of the image content, standard sparse representation classification methods [288] can be outperformed for military vehicle classification on the Comanche IR dataset, which seems to be non-publicly available. The calculation of dense HOGs, however, is expensive and thus slow. An approach that is somehow related to HOGs is presented in [259]: Local Steering Kernels (LSK) are used as low-level descriptors in the LWIR spectrum to capture local image geometry rather than gradient information. The result is a representation of persons that is more robust to image noise and low resolution compared to HOGs. Not only a higher detection rate is achieved but also faster processing time.

Benenson et al. [289] denote Haar-like features, HOGs, and channel features as *hand-crafted* features. This means that a human expert designs or at least strongly influences the way of describing the image content and thus predefines many parameters. On the one hand, this can make sense for training datasets that cannot represent the application environment in its entirety. Then, the training process can profit from the human expert's assistance. On the other hand, this somehow limits the learning capabilities since complex tasks such as person detection under arbitrary conditions may not be captured by a model consisting of few hundred or thousand parameters. The application of deep learning and Deep Convolutional Neural Networks (DCNNs) to the ImageNet challenge in [290] was the most recent milestone in object classification. In contrast to hand-crafted features, deep learning aims at learning as many parameters as possible automatically and purely data-driven. Here, the human expert designs a neural network architecture that usually implements image convolutions within the first layers to map the image content to higher-level representations and thus generate so-called deep features. These convolutional layers can then be followed by fully connected layers that serve as a classifier for the deep features as for example done for the well-known networks AlexNet [290] or VGG-16 [291]. Such a DCNN gets an image as input and outputs class probabilities. As only the structure of the convolution filters within the network is fixed, all network parameters such as the filter weights can be learned from scratch. AlexNet and VGG-16 consist of 60 million and 140 million parameters, respectively. Since DCNN training from scratch needs millions of training samples and can be very time-consuming, the authors provide the model parameters that were achieved after training for the ImageNet challenge. These parameters can be used as an initialization to start for example with meaningful deep features for own DCNN architecture development and training. Recommended further reading about neural networks and deep learning is provided in [292] and [293].

The described DCNN architectures are able to solve the classification problem but not the localization problem. For general object detection, new architectures were introduced that implicitly solve both problems such as Faster Regions with CNN features (R-CNN) by [294], Single Shot MultiBox Detector (SSD) by [295], or You Only Look Once (YOLO) by [296]. YOLO recently even became the state-of-the-art for object detection in applications that require fast runtime. Adapting such multi-class detectors to the domain of person detection, however, is not a trivial task some authors show [297, 298]. This approach of domain adaptation is also known as transfer learning: building up on a Faster R-CNN architecture initialized with the VGG-16 parameters pre-trained with ImageNet, different person detection datasets are used such as Caltech for additional training of the DCNN in order to transfer the domain from general object detection to person detection [299].

Up to this point, deep learning-based person detection was discussed in the VIS spectrum only. Things are getting even more difficult when considering DCNNs for IR person detection as pre-trained models such as AlexNet or VGG-16 are not available for the IR spectrum. The main problem is that public IR datasets that are comparable in its extent to ImageNet or COCO do not exist by now. In recent literature, however, experiments showed that cross-spectral domain adaptation can be a promising approach. Several authors [300–303] start with a neural network initialized with pure VIS parameters and use IR person detection datasets such as CVC-09, KAIST, or the FLIR Thermal Dataset for successful transfer learning. Wagner et al. [300] even extend the amount of training data by utilizing the RGB red channel of the pure VIS Caltech dataset to simulate additional IR person detection data. In [304], however, the authors show that utilizing more and more data for pre-fine-tuning does not always improve the performance. But actually, this might be an effect caused by IR dataset biases or simply too small IR datasets for training since other authors in the VIS spectrum can somehow prove the statement *there's no data like more data* empirically [305]. Further improvement can be achieved by combining real and synthetic training data [169, 306] or by reducing the spectral domain gap using appropriate image pre-processing and model fine-tuning, as proposed in [303]. Such cross-spectral properties can even be learned by a DCNN as shown by [307].

Multi-spectral person detection is of particular interest. Liu et al. [301] expect powerful synergies between the VIS and LWIR spectra: persons are usually more clearly visible at daytime in the VIS spectrum due to the natural illumination but at nighttime in the LWIR spectrum due to the larger temperature differences. By fusing individual VIS and IR networks for person detection, several authors [300–302] designed multi-spectral DCNN architectures that are able to learn these synergies implicitly. Experiments clearly prove the effectiveness of this spectral fusion approach and the improvement of the KAIST training dataset annotations [308, 309] enabled authors to achieve further progress. More complex DCNN architectures use illumination-aware weighting functions in a late fusion strategy [310, 311]. An interesting idea is given in [309], where the alignment error between the VIS and LWIR image pairs of the KAIST dataset is implicitly considered and successfully modeled. Further so-called modality imbalancing problems not only for alignment but also for illumination and feature imbalance are addressed in [312]. All mentioned approaches are highly inspired by Faster R-CNN architectures. The most recent advance is achieved by introducing anchor-free or box-less approaches to the topic of multi-spectral person detection [313]. Such approaches are efficient and specifically well-suited to detect small-scale persons in the image.

Impetus for research is not infrequently provided by the appearance of new datasets. Just like the KAIST dataset revived multi-spectral person detection in 2015, the release of the FLIR Thermal Dataset in 2019 motivated authors to work again on object detection in thermal IR imagery, which is done using novel deep learning techniques [314, 315]. In general, it can be stated that there is still plenty of potential for further improvements in the field of IR and multi-spectral person and object detection using deep learning. This potential can be boosted even more as soon as appropriately improved, extended, or just novel datasets exist for DCNN training.

## 4.3    OBJECT TRACKING

*Object tracking is the process of using sensor measurements to determine the location of one or more objects over time* according to [316]. In visual object tracking, video data is analyzed to propagate the positions of present objects within an observed scene across the consecutive images. Tracking is an essential requirement for surveillance systems in order to interpret the environment [317]. This becomes apparent when considering a system that assists humans in gaining scene understanding and situational awareness: in some cases, complex events and interactions between individual pedestrians, groups of people, or drivers of different vehicles must be recognized before actions or behaviors can be understood and predicted properly. Since observation

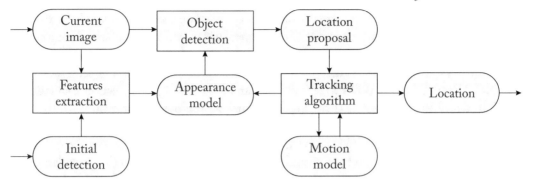

Figure 4.5: Typical processing pipeline for single object tracking.

over time is a crucial aspect toward the development of such a system, the objects participating in a scene must be tracked as precisely as possible to robustly derive further information about the objects, their behavior, and their interactions. But not only video surveillance is an important field of application for object tracking. In robot vision [318] or automated driving [206, 319], object tracking aims at localizing objects to interact with or determining free space for moving. Further applications emerge from video indexing [320] or human-machine interaction such as gesture recognition or eye tracking [321].

Following [322], four aspects characterize an object tracking algorithm: (1) an object representation such as point, bounding box, ellipse, contour, or silhouette; (2) tracking features such as color, edges, optical flow, or texture; (3) an object detection approach such as point detection, background subtraction, or segmentation, and (4) an object tracking algorithm such as point tracking, kernel tracking, or silhouette tracking. Various challenges exist that make visual tracking a difficult task. Variation in object appearance and background is probably the most prominent challenge that can distract a tracking algorithm. Such variations can originate from occlusions, changes in camera view angle, non-rigid object motion, changes in illumination, varying distance between object and camera, or reflections on the object surface. Further challenges arise from poor image quality, low object resolution, confusion due to distracting image content in the background that appears similar to the tracked object, or abrupt changes in object motion. In general, visual object tracking approaches can be subdivided in two categories: Single Object Tracking (SOT) and Multiple Object Tracking (MOT). In Fig. 4.5, a typical SOT processing pipeline is visualized. Each image sequence comes with an initial detection that is often represented by a bounding box. The content of this detection, which is usually an object of interest, should be tracked as precisely as possible across the entire sequence. Features are extracted to model the appearance of the initial detection's image content. This appearance model is used to locate the tracked region within the subsequent images. Using a motion model that for example predicts the track's current location based on a motion history, the proposed location is verified by a tracking algorithm and can be corrected if necessary. Both appearance and motion model can be updated after this step based on the new derived information. As a result, a bounding box in each image of the sequence is provided that marks the current estimated object position or no bounding box at all if the algorithm lost the object. Typical evaluation measures consider the accuracy of tracking such as the f-score or Object Tracking Accuracy (OTA) and Precision (OTP) [249, 323]. Similar to the object detection evaluation measures introduced in Section 4.2, these measures analyze the overlap of ground truth and tracking bounding boxes. Further measures focus on object localization such as Deviation [324] and Position Based Measure (PBM) [325]. Both calculate the distance between the ground truth and object centroid. A comprehensive and recommended survey on SOT is provided in [326]. The currently most popular SOT benchmarks in the VIS spectrum are the Visual Object Tracking (VOT) Challenge [327], the Object Tracking Benchmark (OTB) [328], and the Amsterdam Library of Ordinary Videos (ALOV) [326]. But we can see a rather fast growing number of new emerging tracking datasets in the literature focusing on certain challenges such as long-term tracking [329] or tracking from a UAV [330]. In MOT, multiple objects are tracked simultaneously within the same scene and labeled with unique identifiers (IDs). Just like for SOT, initial bounding boxes for all present objects can be provided and multiple instances of an SOT algorithm can be run. However, a more common approach is to apply object detection for each image independently and feed the resulting detections into the tracking algorithm. This scheme is also called *tracking-by-detection* [331]. In both cases additional challenges occur compared to SOT. Confusing tracked objects due to similar appearance and spatial proximity for example leads to ID switches. If object detections are used, the data association problem appears: finding an unambiguous association between the detections and the already existing tracks can be very challenging [332]. The complexity for standard solutions such as the Hungarian algorithm [333] grows exponentially with the number of tracked objects. Further reading is provided in [334] and [335]. In addition, object detection approaches with bounding boxes as object representation can cause split detections with multiple bounding boxes for one object or merged detections with multiple objects for one bounding box. The temporal context often can help to avoid such mistakes affecting the tracking process. However, proper split and merge handling by the tracking algorithm is necessary in such cases [336, 337]. The evaluation measures f-score, OTA, and OTP as described for SOT can be used for MOT, too. It does make sense, however, to penalize ID switches and thus extend OTA and OTP to Multiple Object Tracking Accuracy (MOTA) and Precision (MOTP) [249, 323]. Further evaluation measures consider entire trajectories of objects instead of accumulating mistakes image by image: Wu et al. [338] consider an object to be *mostly tracked* if 80% or more of its ground truth trajectory is covered. A trajectory coverage of 20% or less is counted as *mostly lost* and in between 20% and 80% it is denoted *partially tracked*. In order to penalize state changes during tracking from tracked to not tracked, the number of *track fragmentations* is incremented for each state change. Further reading about MOT is provided in [339] and [340]. In the VIS spectrum, the MOT Challenge [341, 342] can be used for benchmarking.

Table 4.2: Available public datasets for IR visual object tracking. We distinguish between Single Object Tracking (SOT) and Multiple Object Tracking (MOT) as tracking challenge.

| Dataset | Related Publication | Year | Spectral Bands | Videos | Tracking Challenge |
|---|---|---|---|---|---|
| ETH Thermal Infrared Dataset | [256] | 2014 | LWIR | 8 | MOT |
| Boston University Thermal IR Video Benchmark (BU-TIV) | [348] | 2014 | LWIR | 7 | MOT |
| Linköping Thermal Infrared (LTIR) | [346] | 2015 | LWIR | 20 | SOT |
| Visual Object Tracking Thermal Infrared (VOT-TIR) | [344] | 2016 | LWIR | 25 | MOT |
| Pedestrian Tracking Benchmark Thermal Infrared (PTB-TIR) | [343] | 2018 | LWIR | 60 | MOT |
| Large Scale Object Tracking Benchmark (LSOTB-TIR) | [349] | 2020 | LWIR | 1,400 | SOT |
| Benchmarking IR Dataset for Surveillance with Aerial Intelligence (BIRDSAI) | [352] | 2020 | LWIR | 172 | MOT |
| Maritime Detection, Classification, and Tracking (MarDCT) | [257] | 2015 | VIS, LWIR | 9 | MOT |
| Grayscale Thermal Object Tracking Benchmark (GTOT) | [350] | 2016 | VIS, LWIR | 50 | MOT |
| Singapore Maritime Dataset (SMD) | [258] | 2017 | VIS, NIR | 81 | SOT |
| RGB Thermal (RGBT234) | [146] | 2019 | VIS, LWIR | 234 | SOT |

The number and extent of available public IR datasets for object tracking is limited. Actually, nearly each of the datasets introduced in Table 4.1 of Section 4.2 provides videos, so they could serve as a data basis not only for object detection but also for the evaluation of object tracking. Either missing or insufficient annotation as well as lack of diversity [343], however, disallow the practical usage of these datasets since at least bounding boxes and unique object IDs must be labeled to apply the aforementioned evaluation measures. Due to this fact, only the two multi-spectral maritime datasets MarDCT and SMD from Table 4.1 can be directly used to evaluate MOT without the need for at least partial re-labeling. The SMD dataset is particularly noteworthy due to its extend. It consists of 81 image sequences, of which 63 are fully labeled with 534 individual tracks in total. In addition, there are few IR datasets specifically dedicated to SOT. Table 4.2 shows an overview of the most prominent datasets. The probably most commonly used SOT dataset is the Visual Object Tracking Thermal Infrared (VOT-TIR)

Challenge provided by [344]. In 2016, it consisted of 25 images sequences acquired with 10 different LWIR sensors indoor and outdoor. However, this challenge does not exist as a pure IR challenge anymore, but it was changed to the multi-spectral VOT-RGBT challenge [345]. The Linköping Thermal Infrared (LTIR) dataset introduced in [346] served as a groundwork for the VOT-TIR benchmark since originally back in 2015 the entire LTIR dataset became the data base for the first VOT-TIR challenge [347]. In the meantime, the VOT-TIR dataset was extended in terms of diversity. However, one big benefit of the LTIR dataset still is that the sequences are provided with 8-bit and 16-bit dynamic range, whereas only 8-bit is available in the VOT-TIR dataset. The Boston University Thermal IR Video Benchmark (BU-TIV) [348] consists of five sequences for SOT and MOT of pedestrians as well as two sequences for SOT and MOT of bats. The IR images are provided with 16-bit dynamic range. The ETH Thermal IR Dataset [256] provides eight sequences that can be used to evaluate SOT. The Pedestrian Tracking Benchmark Thermal IR (PTB-TIR) dataset [71] can be used for SOT of pedestrians only. It consists of 60 sequences that were collected from existing datasets such as the OSU Color-Thermal, BU-TIV, or Terravic Motion IR (see Table 4.1) and re-annotated for the SOT task. The currently most promising dataset is the Large-Scale High-Diversity Thermal Infrared Object Tracking Benchmark (LSOTB-TIR) [349]. It consists of 1,400 videos with more than 600,000 frames, which makes it the by far most comprehensive public dataset at this time. The dataset is diverse as it contains five difference object classes person, animal, vehicle, aircraft, and boat and covers four different imaging scenarios: hand-held, drone-mounted, vehicle-mounted, and video surveillance. The used videos were not self-acquired by crawled from the web (e.g., from YouTube). Furthermore, 30 different object tracking approaches were evaluated on the dataset to provide an initial benchmark. Examples images taken from this dataset are shown in Fig. 4.6. The described datasets so far all provide only one spectral band: LWIR. In [350], the multispectral Grayscale Thermal Object Tracking Benchmark (GTOT) for SOT was introduced. There are 50 videos with aligned grayscale VIS and LWIR spectrum. Among these videos are collected ones taken from the OSU Color-Thermal or the LITIV [351] datasets. The very comprehensive RGB-Thermal (RGBT234) [146] SOT dataset consists of 234 aligned VIS and LWIR videos. In contrast to the GTOT dataset, RGBT234 not only contains RGB color information in the VIS spectrum but also provides sequences acquired by moving cameras. The Benchmarking IR Dataset for Surveillance with Aerial Intelligence (BIRDSAI) [352] was acquired in South Africa and contains aerial videos in the LWIR spectrum showing humans and animals. It consists of 48 real and 124 synthetic videos with 62,000 real and 100,000 synthetic images in total. In addition to track id and location, the GT labels contain the class and even the species.

In the remainder of this section, the focus lies on SOT. The main reason is that there is no significant difference between MOT in the VIS and the IR spectrum. MOT usually expects already given detections. Hence, the difference between VIS and IR in MOT emerges from the object detection approach. On the contrary, SOT does not rely on any object detections

Figure 4.6: Example images taken from the Large-Scale High-Diversity Thermal Infrared Object Tracking Benchmark (LSOTB-TIR) [349]. The dataset is diverse and large with 1,400 videos acquired in four different scenarios and five different object classes.

and thus the tracking algorithms can be considered class-agnostic and usually utilize appearance information mainly. In their comprehensive survey, [326] consider the VIS spectrum only. They distinguish between two classes of tracking algorithms: (1) tracking using matching and (2) tracking using discriminative classification. In tracking using matching, an object model is built from previous frame(s) and matched against the current frame to localize the object of interest. A simple model can comprise the pixel intensity values inside the initial bounding box. Such a model is often called *template*. Then, the Normalized Cross-Correlation (NCC) can be used to match the template with candidate regions in the current frame sampled around the previous object location [353]. This simple but still effective approach is particularly suitable for small sized objects that cover only few pixels within the image. Instead of pixel intensity values, Comaniciu et al. [354] use histograms as an object model in their famous mean shift tracking approach. Many other methods exist that introduce extended appearance models or constraints such as sparse representation [355] for higher robustness against object appearance changes. Tracking using discriminative classification aims at learning a model for the distinction of the foreground, which is the object of interest, against the background. Therefore, a classifier such as RF or SVM is trained with samples from the previous frame(s) and used to distinguish between object and background pixels. Prominent approaches are Multiple Instance Learning (MIL) tracking [356], Structured Output Learning with Kernels (STRUCK) [357], and Kernelized Correlation Filters (KCF) [358]. Especially correlation filter-based approaches gathered attention within the last years due to their simplicity and fast processing speed with several hundred frames per second [359]. With the introduction of deep learning, existing methods such as correlation filters were improved using stronger features for tracking [360] but also end-to-end trainable DCNN architectures were proposed such as Siamese CNNs [361, 362].

Most authors in recent literature about IR SOT use the thermal IR spectrum as it is well-suited for 24/7 surveillance without any active illumination. There are applications for the NIR spectrum such as eye and gaze tracking [363, 364] and the SWIR spectrum such as missile tracking [365, 366], but only very few papers and articles exist. Hence, we continue with discussing approaches for thermal IT SOT. Following [367] and [368], there are several challenges: objects are usually small within the image, which is the result of low IR camera resolution and large distance between the camera and the observed objects in typical surveillance applications. However, descriptors such as HOG or deep features that are popular in VIS SOT require sufficient object resolution to achieve discriminative power. Furthermore, thermal IR images are often affected by noise, do not provide color information, are less textured, and differently preprocessed across different IR cameras. In order to deeply analyze the differences between SOT in VIS and thermal IR videos, Gundogdu et al. [367] use two multi-spectral datasets and apply adopted SOT algorithms developed for VIS imagery such as MIL, STRUCK, or Minimum Output Sum of Squared Error (MOSSE) [369]. A first experiment shows that feature-based discriminative tracking algorithms are much more sensitive to the imaging spectrum than template matching based approaches. Hence, a novel tracking approach is proposed that tries to overcome the spectral gap. It is an ensemble tracking algorithm consisting of multiple MOSSE trackers, which use NCC to match appearance models. The basic idea is that each tracker captures one object appearance as a template and applies L1 projection to decide, which of the trackers currently fits best and thus is activated for tracking the object. This method is denoted TBOOST and performs superior on IR imagery in comparison to eight tracking algorithms adopted from VIS SOT in terms of success rate and precision. This performance gap is even bigger for small-sized objects in the images. STRUCK appears to have the highest cross-spectral generalization capability. Similar to [367], Berg et al. [368] discuss the differences between tracking in the VIS and the IR spectrum and aim at designing a thermal IR specific SOT algorithm. This approach uses template matching based on distribution fields [370], where each template pixel is represented by a probability distribution such as a local histogram. Motivated by [371], channel coded vectors are used instead of local histograms [368]. In addition, three improvements specifically for thermal IR SOT are proposed. (1) Not only the object template is modeled by channel coded vectors but also the surrounding background in order to achieve higher robustness against a changing scene background. (2) An adaptive object region is defined that chooses an inner region of the tracking template assuming that this inner region provides more stable information for tracking compared to the outer regions. (3) Finally, object scale changes are detected and handled. The resulting tracker ranks 4th in the VOT-TIR 2015 challenge, in which the correlation filter based approach Spatially Regularized Discriminatively learned Correlation Filters (SRDCF) ranked 1st. Unfortunately, no comparison to the IR specific tracking approach in [367] is given. Besides the multi-spectral GTOT dataset, the authors in [350] present collaborative sparse representation integrated into a Bayesian filtering framework for multi-spectral object tracking. Sparse representations coefficients are calculated individually for the VIS and the LWIR spectrum and then fused on this coefficients level. In contrast to related literature, this fusion does not assume that each spectrum contributes equally to the tracking approach. This appears to be intuitive since usually not both spectra offer utilizable features for tracking simultaneously. Instead, the sparse representation and a spectral weighting are jointly optimized. In an extensive evaluation, 13 different tracking algorithms mostly adopted from the VIS spectrum such as KCF, MIL, or STRUCK are evaluated with the proposed one performing best with respect to various performance measures.

As mentioned in Section 4.2, deep learning and DCNNs are not easily transferable from the VIS to the IR spectrum without appropriate transfer learning. This is the case not only for object detection but also for object tracking. Deep learning for thermal IR SOT is analyzed in [372] with the result that DCNNs trained end-to-end for VIS SOT are not suitable to be transferred to the IR spectrum. Instead, deep features as they can be picked from the last convolutional layers of DCNNs (also called encoder network) represent the object appearance in a highly discriminative way and indeed can be re-used for IR SOT. They are embedded into two promising correlation filter based tracking frameworks: SRDCF and Discriminative Scale Space Tracker (DSST). Hand-crafted features such as HOG are outperformed by the deep features. Furthermore, in terms of expected overlap DSST with deep features shows superior performance. This is noteworthy since SRDCF achieved the best results in VOT and VOT-TIR 2015 but can be outperformed by the combination of DSST and deep features. Just like [372], the authors in [373] propose deep features for thermal IR tracking introducing the Multi-layer Convolutional Features (MCFTS). Deep features from multiple convolutional layers are embedded into a correlation filter based framework. An ensemble of weak trackers is applied to generate feature response maps and the fusion of these maps is used to predict the object location in the current image. Furthermore, scale changes of the tracked object are considered while analyzing the feature response maps. The results on the VOT-TIR challenge 2015 are promising but the correlation filter based tracking approach by [359] originally developed for the VIS spectrum outperforms the proposed tracker in the VOT-TIR challenge 2016. In order to overcome the issue of not having a sufficient amount of training data, in [374] a Generative Adversarial Network (GAN) is used to hallucinate thermal IR images from a large-scale VIS SOT dataset. With this training data, a DCNN learns to extract deep features for a correlation filter based tracking approach. The IR features learned on the hallucinated data clearly outperform the IR features learned on the comparatively small real IR training dataset. In [375], a Multi-task Matching Network (MMNet) is proposed to extract thermal IR specific deep features. The neural network extracts discriminative features and fine-grained correlation features simultaneously and can thus achieve higher robustness for thermal IR SOT. Just recently, Siamese DCNN architectures became popular for object tracking in thermal IR videos. In contrast to the rather classification-based tracking approaches discussed so far that consider inter-class differences, the authors in [376] and [377] propose a verification-based approach that tries to measure the similarity between arbitrary objects and hence focus on intra-class differences. This is modeled in a Siamese DCNN architecture that can be trained end-to-end. The results on VOT-TIR 2015 and 2016 are convincing. Furthermore, multi-spectral RGB-T tracking approaches are gaining attention by the community [378, 379] and even made the famous VOT challenge include a separate RGB-T challenge since 2019.

MOT in thermal IR is usually based on initial detections produced by independent motion detection algorithms such as background subtraction [256, 260, 380, 381] or keypoint detection [382]. Detectors such as template matching or HOG SVM can refine the detected motion regions [256, 381]. MOT can then be performed by solving the data association problem only [380] or improved by introducing additional motion models such as Kalman Filter [383] or Particle Filter [260]. Further reading about independent motion detection as well as MOT using stationary or moving cameras is provided by [384].

## 4.4   OTHERS

In this section, we discuss further tasks for image and video content analysis that are present in the VIS domain but are not (yet) actively researched in the IR spectrum. We focus on tasks where at least few literature about utilizing IR images exists.

**Semantic Segmentation**: Probably one of the most interesting tasks is semantic segmentation. The goal is to assign a semantic label to each pixel in the image. The set of labels contains classes like person, vehicle, building, vegetation, sky, or street. However, higher-level information about object instances or boundaries is usually not considered. The most common evaluation metrics are calculated pixelwise: f-score or Jaccard index, if the class distribution is ignored during evaluation, and the mean Average Precision (mAP) otherwise. This task became a hot topic in the computer vision community with the introduction of deep learning [385, 386]. DCNNs improved the performance by leaps and bounds compared to approaches built up on other classifiers such as random forests [387]. Popular applications for semantic segmentation are autonomous driving [388], where a self-driving car can create a fine-grained representation of its surrounding environment, or medical imaging [389, 390], where semantic labels can for example indicate tumor cells in Magnetic Resonance Imaging (MRI) data. But why is semantic segmentation not yet popular for IR computer vision? In order to assign a class label to each pixel, semantic segmentation analyzes the texture of an image region surrounding the pixel of interest. Therefore, the presence of texture is needed obviously. Hence, the potential of thermal IR images to serve as a source of data for semantic segmentation is directly diminished as they are usually significantly less textured compared to VIS, NIR, or SWIR images as seen for example in Fig. 1.4. However, NIR and SWIR cameras are less popular for automotive applications as they do not provide a sufficiently new source of data in addition to VIS cameras on the one hand and as they are still too expensive (esp. SWIR). Thermal IR cameras, however, are becoming increasingly popular for automotive applications as we can see in the vital community for multi-spectral pedestrian detection for example [63]. When having a look at the few recent literature on semantic segmentation for IR images [391, 392], it can be seen that adopting approaches from the VIS domain like SegNet [385] is a well-performing baseline. But even after fine-tuning DC-NNs to the IR domain, the performance is not comparable to VIS images. This is probably due to the lack of visible texture and fine object structure in IR images. The authors of the cited papers aim at compensating for this drawback of IR images by incorporating edge prior knowledge to inject a gated feature-wise transform layer into their Edge-Conditioned CNN (EC-CNN) or by introducing a deep feature enhancement module to reduce typical artifacts of thermal IR images like blur or low resolution. Both approaches are built up on DCNN architectures taken from the VIS domain. Public datasets like the Segment Objects in Day And night (SODA) and the Low-resolution Far-infrared Pedestrian Dataset (LFPD) are mentioned in the papers but they do not seem to be publicly available, yet, at least not for a direct download on a dedicated website. However, existing multi-spectral datasets [150, 393] can be utilized for this task, too, of course. In general, multi-spectral approaches for semantic segmentation [150, 393, 394] show promising results as VIS and thermal IR images can contain complementing information as already discussed for person detection in Section 4.2. Hence, more robust solutions to challenging scenarios can be obtained such as limited visibility at night, adverse weather conditions, or similar color and pattern in the objects contained in the scene. Some authors reduce the complexity by focusing segmentation on only few classes of interest such as pedestrians [395, 396]. It is expected that the number of cross- and multi-spectral applications will keep growing during next years due to the number of platforms already available—for instance, most of new mobile devices are equipped with cameras from different spectral bands such as NIR and VIS. Finally, it should be mentioned that high-quality, cooled thermal IR cameras can produce images with much more detailed textures and structures due to the higher sensitivity to temperature differences. But such cameras are still way too expensive for most applications nowadays.

**Action Recognition**: Action recognition is the task of automatically understanding human behavior and actions in videos. According to [397], human behavior can occur at different levels of complexity such as gestures, actions, interactions, or group activities. Often, the action's mean duration grows with a higher complexity. A usual approach for action recognition is the extraction of spatio-temporal features from an image sequence and a subsequent classification [398]. Classification can be done using either traditional machine learning approaches [399] or deep learning techniques [400]. Among the most prominent challenges are spotting an action within a video and segmenting its temporal length [401], finding a suitable representation for spatio-temporal features [402], and achieving viewpoint invariance [403]. Typical applications are automatic video captioning, human-machine interfaces, or video surveillance. Just like in semantic segmentation and other computer vision tasks, approaches from the VIS spectrum are adopted and adapted for their application to the thermal IR spectrum. The appearance of humans looks different in thermal IR compared to VIS but approaches for action recognition are expected to work similarly though. As mentioned by [404], one of the main benefits in using IR videos is the robustness to shadows and to weak or changing illumination. In older literature such as [405], the authors adopt the quite famous approach called Motion Energy Images (MEI) and Motion History Images (MHI) by [406] for spatio-temporal feature representation and modify it to Silhouette Energy Images (SEI). Nowadays, authors use standard methods like Hidden Markov Models (HMMs) as proposed by [404] or DCNNs with 3D convolutions to capture the temporal information [407, 408]. Other methods include additional modalities in the DCNN like optical flow [409] or salience [410]. There are also some cross-spectral based action recognition approaches. In [411], the authors propose a strategy to adapt action recognition from VIS spectrum images to LWIR images showing the potential to perform cross-spectral action recognition. More recently, in [412] a novel representation is proposed to tackle the missing data in cross-spectral action recognition approaches. This representation is obtained through a neural network referred to as Partial-modal Generative Adversarial Network (PM-GANs). Just like in [307], the network learns to generate a full-modal representation using data from only partial modalities. The approach is evaluated with a paired LWIR and VIS spectrum dataset for action recognition. Finally, there are few public datasets available: Infrared Action Recognition (InfAR) [413], IITR Infrared Action Recognition (IITR-IAR) [410], and Virat [414] are datasets that can be used for human action recognition in the thermal IR spectrum.

Other related work is tackling the tasks of hand gesture recognition [415] or room occupancy estimation [416]. Finally, contact-less biometric human identification and analysis using thermal IR images is still a niche topic, but has the potential to gain more attention within the next years. In the literature, we can find approaches for vein pattern recognition [417, 418], fever detection [419], ear recognition [420], or fingerprint recognition [421].

C H A P T E R   5

# Applications

The entire content of this book is quite strongly application-oriented. However, in this chapter, we highlight some relevant and popular applications that highly benefit from utilizing IR imagery. We aim to build to bridge from rather traditional IR based applications such as Automatic Target Recognition (ATR) or video surveillance on the one hand to rather modern applications such as biometrics and autonomous vehicles on the other. Within each individual application we try to answer questions like *What is the benefit of using IR imagery in this context?* or *What are the key differences between VIS and IR image information in this application?* At the same time, we have to skip several popular applications that would go too far beyond the scope of this book. Among them is remote sensing, where satellites are used to observe the earth often equipped with hyperspectral cameras that operate in the IR spectrum. Such satellites analyze vegetation, monitor cities, or support disaster monitoring. Further applications skipped here are visual inspection and medical computer vision. Each of these three topics has its own active community together with well-discussed literature and benchmarking datasets.

## 5.1    AUTOMATIC TARGET RECOGNITION (ATR)

Automatic Target Recognition (ATR) is a computer vision task that originally comes from the IR domain. This is in contrast to all the other tasks presented in this book that were introduced for VIS imagery first and then adopted for IR imagery. Other popular modalities for ATR are Synthetic Aperture Radar (SAR) and hyper-spectral imaging [422]. The goal is to detect and recognize objects in a large distance using long-range thermal IR or combined VIS/IR cameras and to identify them as objects of interest. But ATR can go even further analyzing activities and motion patterns to detect anomalies in these patterns. Wide-angle VIS/IR sensing platforms are used that can cover an area larger than 1 km$^2$ for aerial, maritime, or ground-based surveillance. Such remote sensing applications often face the challenge of observing objects at low resolution in highly cluttered scenes as seen in Fig. 5.1. Hence, they are substantially more challenging for exploitation algorithms to generate low numbers of false positive and false negative detections when fielded in operational theaters with real-time requirements.

In general, the term recognition can cover both detection or classification. So, there is some work on ATR focusing on the detection of hot objects such as missiles or airplanes in a large distance using thermal IR imagery. This can be considered as detecting saliency based on the temperature difference as a feature. The challenge is to detect an object covering only few pixels within the image often against the sky. In addition to the tiny object appearance without clear

Figure 5.1: Sample images from SENSIAC ATR Database (left) and VIRAT [414] (right) datasets for classification and activity recognition of small targets of interest. The left image shows a tank in several kilometers of distance from the camera.

shape or texture, image noise and background clutter such as clouds make robust object detection very difficult. In recent literature, appropriate filtering and adaptive thresholding techniques are applied to solve the problem [423–425]. Even though the objects of interest are very small, deep learning-based approaches are proposed to distinguish between true positive detections and clutter. Therefore, proposals are generated using adaptive thresholding, sliding windows, or salient feature detection such as corners [426]. The proposals are then classified by DCNNs with only few convolutional layers to avoid vanishing of the object inside its receptive field. Such networks are also called *shallow*. A highly recommendable paper on this topic was published by Dai et al. [427]. Together with their paper, they released the first public benchmark dataset for small IR target detection: the Single-frame InfraRed Small Target (SIRST) Benchmark that comes with 427 images containing 480 labeled point-like object instances.

Further challenging and active research topics in ATR are the classification and activity recognition of such low-resolution and small-scaled targets in cluttered and visually degraded environment. The (obviously) extremely uncooperative behavior of observed objects in the scene that try to camouflage themselves further complicates these tasks. Salient thermal IR signatures, however, often provide a better source of data for ATR in comparison to VIS images: examples signatures of military vehicles taken from the SENSIAC ATR Database[1] are shown in Fig. 5.2. The dataset contains VIS and MWIR sequences that include imagery of civilian and military ground vehicles maneuvering around a closed-circular path at ranges from 1–3 km. In the figure, we can see two different vehicles at a distance of 1 km. We show each vehicle in side and front view. Furthermore, there are VIS and MWIR images at daytime and MWIR images at nighttime. VIS images at nighttime are not included in the dataset. We can see that the scenes

---

[1]https://www.dsiac.org/resources/available-databases/atr-algorithm-development-image-database (last accessed: August 23, 2021).

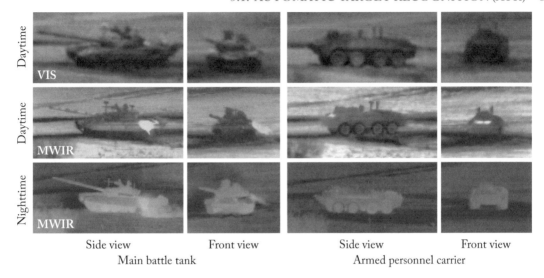

Figure 5.2: Example images taken from the SENSIAC ATR Database that show military vehicle signatures in the VIS and the MWIR spectrum at a distance of 1 km. Especially at nighttime, objects are obviously more visible in the MWIR compared to the VIS spectrum.

in the two spectra VIS and MWIR are not so different visually during the day. The reason is that the vehicles are darker than their surrounding environment in the VIS spectrum and the ground is warmer than the vehicles in the MWIR spectrum. Bright regions in the MWIR images indicate hot vehicle regions such as the engine or the exhaust plume. The ground is getting colder at night, which causes the thermal IR signatures to appear more prominently in the nighttime MWIR images. Another visible finding is that the side view offers more distinctive features compared to the front view such as wheels, tank chains, or armament.

With this closer look at Fig. 5.2, we can get an idea, why ATR usually is a more challenging computer vision task than for example video surveillance that is discussed in the next section of this chapter. While video surveillance needs to raise an alarm in case of an abnormal event such as intruding or fighting, ATR has to precisely localize and classify the present object. ATR operates at higher distances between camera and observed scene. Furthermore, a variety of different object classes must be supported, while video surveillance is often just focused on humans or cars. One could even say that video surveillance is a special case of ATR. However, since ATR is usually military oriented, it is less price-driven. Hence, high-end, cooled-thermal IR cameras are used in ATR and provide a much better image quality and thermal resolution compared to uncooled IR cameras typically used in video surveillance.

Automatically exploiting such scenes as presented in Fig. 5.1 can be done by utilizing the approaches described in Chapter 4: change detection, object detection, classification, and tracking. Comprehensive overviews of ATR in general and related processing algorithms are provided by Hammoud et al. [428] and Sadjadi et al. [429]. One of the most discussed topics is the lack of data for algorithm development and evaluation. Usually, there are only few images or videos available from the targets so that machine learning algorithms have to be supported by augmented or synthetic training samples. In this context, Yu et al. [430] distinguish between data-driven approaches that utilize real-world training data and model-driven approaches that entirely learn from synthetic data such as Computer-Aided Design (CAD) models. To tackle the problem of being viewpoint invariant, manifolds can be used as a representation for multi-view shape modeling of 3D CAD models [431]. For the same problem, synthetic images can be used to train a DCNN that can achieve state-of-the-art performance on real ATR data [432]. To tackle the issue of insufficiently labeled data for the training process of DCNNs for aerial ATR applications, limited available real-world collections of aerial targets of interest (e.g., tanks, launchers, etc.) can be augmented to generate synthetic IR imagery using tools like Digital Imaging and Remote Sensing Image Generation (DIRSIG) from targets' 3D CAD models [433]. In this way, a VIS/IR sensing platform is simulated in various operational environmental conditions (e.g., day, night, covered target, cluttered background, etc.). A similar approach is chosen in [19] to enhance the variation of synthetic training images by adding noise, blur, or different weather conditions in order to train a more robust DCNN. While such synthetic data is easy to generate and does not require human labeling for training DCNNs, simulating realistic noise, occlusions, and background clutters remains a big challenge. Because of such training data requirements by deep learning techniques, the traditional phase-correlation template-based ATR and related manifold-based shape generative modeling techniques [434] remain applicable today with reasonable performance.

Exploiting Full-Motion Video (FMV) collected from aerial platform, Hammoud et al. [435] first register captured IR imagery to base satellite maps to enable mapping between pixels in imagery and map locations (geo-registration). Then frame-to-frame registration is performed followed by moving object detection and supervised and unsupervised activity recognition afterwards. For classification, traditional features such as Histograms of Oriented Gradients (HOG) can be used in combination with a Support Vector Machine (SVM) classifier to categorize targets into persons, vehicles, and others [287]. Garagic et al. [436] proposed a generic probabilistic pattern learning and classification framework for a long-range dismounts (humans) activities classification (e.g., digging, running, getting into car, etc.) using a new class of hierarchical Bayesian learning algorithms for efficiently discovering recurring patterns (classes of dismounts) in multiple simultaneous sensor modalities. In [437], a system is proposed that is able to analyze such VIR and IR video data for content-based retrieval from large surveillance video archives. The VIRAT [414] dataset is used to demonstrate the capabilities of the system.

In contrast to FMV, airborne Wide Area Motion Imagery (WAMI) sensors are able to cover a much larger ground area of several tens of square kilometers at a resolution that enables appropriate algorithms to detect and track thousands of moving ground objects such as vehicles [222, 223] or even walking pedestrians [438]. Early sensors of this kind date back to 2013 with the ARGUS-IS platform that can cover 15 square miles in a single imagery.[2] Multiple approaches were proposed to detect motion on the ground and employ multiple object tracking to extract the trajectories of all moving ground vehicles either based on traditional algorithm engineering [439, 440] or deep learning [441, 442]. Based on these trajectories, the moving objects' pattern of life can be determined [443] enabling the detection of outlier trajectories, specific activities, or abnormal behavior.

## 5.2    VIDEO SURVEILLANCE

Video surveillance is an application with great diversity. We can think of typical indoor scenarios, where airports, train stations, or public buildings in general are protected against criminal or terrorist activities. Other use cases in a more private environment aim to prevent burglary or spying. Among the common operational scenarios for outdoor video surveillance there are the protection of borders and critical infrastructure such as harbors or power plants or the defense of military camps against intruders. Detecting suspicious behavior in public places such as digging or fighting is another relevant task. Multiple public datasets provide representative videos together with related ground truth annotations for the just mentioned use cases: videos of persons moving around in buildings or leaving a backpack or other potentially dangerous objects in public places are provided in the CDnet 2014 dataset [210] that was discussed in Section 4.1. The VIRAT dataset [414] contains various human behavioral patterns observed by aerial cameras. One of the first and most popular video surveillance datasets is the Performance Evaluation of Tracking and Surveillance (PETS) benchmark [444]. It has been around for about twenty years now and together with the related workshop[3] it served and serves as an inspiration for many scientists and engineers. Further datasets can be found in Section 4.2, Table 4.1. The aforementioned video surveillance tasks need robust approaches for object detection, classification, tracking, and re-identification. A rather special property of video surveillance is the existence of a camera network consisting of multiple cameras mounted at multiple different locations with different viewing angles. Such camera networks are often used to monitor large infrastructures such as airports that cannot be overseen with a single camera. Special Multi-Target Multi-Camera (MTMC) tracking approaches are needed to re-identify humans or objects across the different cameras. The Duke MTMC Dataset [445] used to be the benchmark dataset for this task but it was retracted in 2019 by the authors due to the violation of privacy rights of the recorded persons.

In general, privacy is an important topic in video surveillance: to protect humans or infrastructure from criminal activities it is necessary to monitor each relevant object in a scene since we never can know, which object acts illegally or endangering at a certain point in time. At the same time, however, it is mandatory to protect the privacy of the monitored persons to

---

[2]Video showing the capabilities of ARGUS-IS: https://www.youtube.com/watch?v=QGxNyaXfJsA (last accessed: August 23, 2021).

[3]http://www.cvg.reading.ac.uk/PETS2021/index.html (last accessed: August 22, 2021).

Figure 5.3: Two example image pairs taken from [15] demonstrating that thermal IR (here: LWIR) implicitly preserves human privacy by providing appearance information that makes person re-identification very difficult for a human.

avoid any kind of general suspicion and to build public trust in video surveillance systems. One option is to apply visual abstractions to surveillance videos in order to represent humans not by their appearance but just by their pose as a skeleton or avatar [446]. In this way, action recognition can be performed preserving the privacy by unveiling the human identity just in case of a verified threat. But still we need to trust the system in a way that the human identity redaction is properly working and switched on. This is, where thermal IR imaging enters the game: MWIR and LWIR images provide appearance information that makes person re-identification very difficult for a human [447]. The reason is that texture information is likely to get lost during IR imaging if the observed object is uniformly tempered, which is often the case for a human face. As a result, the human identity is implicitly redacted. At the beginning, this may sound like a paradox when considering that in Section 5.3 we will discuss IR face recognition. However, Fig. 5.3 shows example image pairs that reinforce this statement. Due to the lack of texture, we need high-resolution face images to identify a human in thermal IR images. This is not given in standard video surveillance scenarios, where persons usually cover just a small fraction of the image.

There is a second aspect that makes thermal IR imaging important for video surveillance: salience. Surveillance scenarios often take place in uncooperative environments. This means that suspects try to hide in the dark or behind other objects. Furthermore, in case of long-range observation, the image resolution of monitored objects is usually very low and thus the visual information may not be sufficient for a human to follow the observed object across the scene. Again this is, where thermal IR imaging is beneficial compared to VIS: due to the temperature difference between humans or man-made objects such as vehicles compared to their surrounding environment, they produce an implicitly salient object signature in MWIR and LWIR images. Two examples are given in Fig. 5.4. The upper image pair was acquired at nighttime and shows persons that are insufficiently illuminated and partially occluded. The lower image pair was acquired at daytime and we can see a highly textured scene with multiple pedestrians. In both

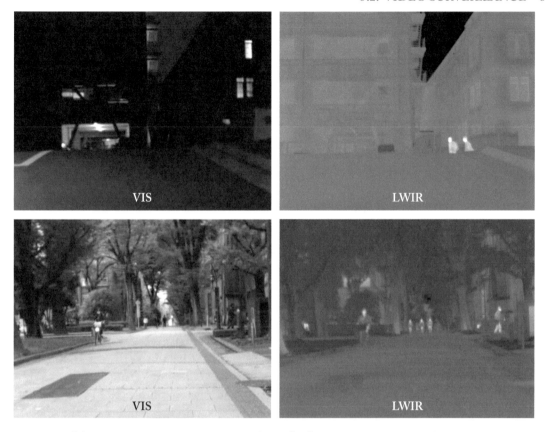

Figure 5.4: Two example image pairs taken from [15] demonstrating that thermal IR imagery (here: LWIR) produces salient signatures for persons that are much easier to spot in the LWIR image on the right compared to the related VIS image on the left.

cases, it is highly challenging in the VIS images to spot all the humans in the scene. They are either invisible due to the absence of reflected light or they merge together with their environment. The related LWIR images greatly support the detection of all humans in the scene due to their prominent IR signature as a result of the temperature difference between objects and scene. This is why thermal IR imaging became popular in video surveillance many years ago already [253, 254]. Finally, as already discussed in Section 4.2, we want to emphasize that approaches for multi-spectral object detection can perfectly benefit from the orthogonal information of texture in the VIS and saliency as well as contours in the thermal IR spectra.

A rather special topic is the observation and identification of people, who illegally ignite pyrotechnics for example in a stadium or anywhere else in order to cover themselves. Usually, the identification of such people is very difficult or even impossible as they are fully covered by fog while burning the pyrotechnics. In such a case, it can be beneficial to use IR cameras that are capable of looking through fog and haze such as SWIR cameras. Together with laser gated viewing technologies that actively illuminate the scene for a given distance range through the fog, the mentioned capability can be even amplified. A good example of powerful SWIR laser gated viewing for this application is presented in [448]. In comparison to VIS or thermal IR imagery, the SWIR camera provides much better visual information to unveil the actions and the human identities behind the fog.

## 5.3   BIOMETRICS AND FACE RECOGNITION

The automated visual analysis of human faces covers various topics such as detection of faces or eyes, verification and identification of faces or eyes, recognition of facial expressions, or estimation of head poses or line of gaze. There are many applications, in which such an analysis plays a key role. The probably most prominent one is biometrics. In [449], it is stated that *biometrics is the science of recognizing the identity of a person based on the physical or behavioral attributes of the individual such as face, fingerprints, voice, and iris*. According to [450] and [451] it can be used to give registered and authorized individuals access to buildings, mobile devices such as laptops, or even vehicles. Some authors [452, 453] emphasize the utilization of biometrics for forensic search, law enforcement, or surveillance tasks such as airport security. But with a rising danger of spoofing within such applications, it can be shown that the LWIR and NIR spectral bands can be effectively used in addition to VIS to uncover face spoofing attacks [454, 455]. Another important application besides biometrics is human-machine interaction. In [456] and [457], the authors discuss the topic of facial expression recognition giving robots the opportunity to understand human intentions and feelings in order to properly respond to them. Furthermore, NIR and LWIR spectral bands can be used to improve head pose tracking and eye-gaze estimation [1, 458–460].

In this section, we will mainly focus on face recognition, which is the most discussed one among the mentioned topics. In the literature, face recognition is considered as an umbrella term for certain, more specific problems such as face verification or face identification. While face verification is the challenge of determining if two images contain the same person, face identification aims at unambiguously ascertaining the identity of a shown person [461]. In [462], face recognition is described as a pipeline that consists of (1) face detection, (2) face alignment, (3) face representation, and (4) face classification. The result of face detection is usually a bounding box that surrounds the face but potentially is not well centered or does not contain the entire face or too much background. This is improved during face alignment by repositioning the bounding box and optimizing image cropping. The face is then represented by a set of extracted features that unambiguously describe the individual appearance of the face. Classification implies that we already have a database with a certain number of classes, which here means different identities of individuals, and from which we aim to find the correct one given a query face. This, however, leads to the quite popular closed-set assumption that all in-

Table 5.1: Available public datasets for IR face recognition

| Dataset | Publication | Year | Spectral Bands | Subjects |
|---|---|---|---|---|
| ND-Collection C | [137] | 2003 | LWIR | 241 |
| Terravic Facial IR Database | [254] | 2006 | LWIR | 20 |
| CBSR NIR Face Dataset | [468] | 2007 | NIR | 197 |
| IIT Delhi Near IR Face Database V2.0 | [473] | 2008 | NIR | 102 |
| PolyU Near-Infrared Face Database | [471] | 2010 | NIR | 335 |
| ND-Collection X1 | [137] | 2003 | VIS, NIR | 82 |
| IRIS Thermal/Visible Face Database | [467] | 2005 | VIS, LWIR | 32 |
| SCface—Surveillance Cameras Face Database | [470] | 2011 | VIS, NIR | 130 |
| USTC Natural Visible and Infrared Facial Expression (NVIE) Database | [472] | 2013 | VIS, NIR | 103 |
| CASIA NIR-VIS 2.0 Database | [474] | 2013 | VIS, NIR | 725 |
| Near-Infrared and Visible Light Face (NIVL) | [469] | 2015 | VIS, NIR | 574 |
| BRSU Multispectral Skin/Face Database | [475] | 2015 | VIS, SWIR | 120 |
| Tufts Face Database | [148] | 2020 | VIS, NIR, LWIR | 113 |

dividuals to be queried already exist within the database. In real-world scenarios, it is usually more common to have an open-set setting with queries of individuals that cannot be assumed to be part of the database already. Hence, the problem becomes much more complex as described for example in [463]. When talking about face recognition, we look at the problem from a pure technical point of view: how can individual faces be represented within an appropriate feature space and how can they be distinguished from each other?

An overview of the currently available IR or multi-spectral public datasets for face recognition is given in Table 5.1. The first datasets in LWIR and NIR spectrum listed here were published in the year 2003. Besides the related publication, we also point out the year, the used spectral bands, and the number of individual subjects within each dataset. We assume that the latter one represents the dataset's comprehensiveness. If more than one spectral band is mentioned, each subject is represented in each band and data fusion approaches or cross-spectral evaluation can be applied. Example images taken from the multi-spectral Tufts Face Database [148] are shown in Fig. 5.5. While the thermal IR bands dominate Tables 4.1 and 4.2, two different IR spectral bands occur frequently here in Table 5.1: NIR and LWIR. Since NIR is adjacent to the VIS band, the appearance of subjects does not change as significantly as it does for the thermal

Figure 5.5: Example images taken from the Tufts Face Database [148] showing the same person's face in multiple spectra.

LWIR band. As a result, similar approaches as for the VIS band can be applied to the NIR spectrum since similar facial features are visible. Mian [464] states that even the same CCD sensors can be used as they are sensitive to both VIS and NIR and with minor modifications, a VIS camera can be made NIR sensitive. It can be stated as a disadvantage that NIR just like VIS requires active illumination in the absence of sunlight. But while artificial light can cause shading that significantly affects the recognition performance in the VIS spectrum, the NIR band is much less sensitive to illumination changes as confirmed several authors [465, 466]. In addition, face recognition can be performed under controlled condition easier as the human eye is insensitive to NIR illumination [468]. In many surveillance or military applications, however, we even want to completely avoid active illumination and thus the thermal LWIR band can be beneficial for face recognition. Although some authors [476] conclude that good-quality LWIR images are superior to VIS images for face recognition, there are some important limitations such as the sensitivity to the environment's and the subject's temperature or the opaqueness of eyeglasses for LWIR imagery [16]. Furthermore, a precise radiometric calibration is mandatory and needs to be done frequently as each calibration degrades over time [477]. However, features that are mostly invariant to the just mentioned limitations and hence can be used for face recognition instead are facial vascular networks or blood perfusion [454, 478, 479]. Vascular networks can even be used to register and face images of the same face over time to perform for example facial tissue tracking [480]. The motivation is that physiological information on the face such as breath extracted from thermal IR images and videos can serve as a biometric [481]. Even a multimodal dataset was published that contains such physiological information acquired by an LWIR camera. This video data together with other collected data can be used to analyze the inattentiveness and the distraction of a driver in road traffic [482].

The BRSU Multispectral Skin/Face Database stands out within the datasets collected in Table 5.1. It is the only dataset that specifically covers the SWIR band. Moreover, the SWIR spectrum is further divided into certain sub-bands to tackle not only the challenge of face recognition but also material classification. Analyzing different SWIR sub-bands for face recognition can be a promising approach, too, as demonstrated in [483]. The list of datasets in Table 5.1 does not make the claim to be complete. Several more IR face recognition datasets are mentioned in the literature [16, 148]. Unfortunately, some of them such as the quite popular Equinox Human Identification at a Distance Database and the IRIS-M3 multi-spectral dataset seem to be not available anymore.

When measuring face recognition performance, it is necessary to understand the most common evaluation protocols applied in current literature. According to [484], face recognition can be evaluated as an identification problem or a verification problem. Face identification can be interpreted as an image retrieval problem, where a query face image is given and compared to a database if face images that contains at least one image of the query individual. The result of this query is a list of images taken from the database that is ranked by the similarity confidence. Then, the quantitative evaluation can be done with respect to this ranking. The Rank-1 and Rank-10 identification rates report, if at least one correct database image was ranked first or ranked among the first ten list entries. This information can be plotted in the Cumulative Match Characteristics Curve (CMC), which gives us the probability that a correct database image is chosen by Rank-$K$. Instead, face verification is treated as a classification problem. Each subject is considered as one class and each image of this subject is one sample of this class. Just like any other classification problem, the quantitative evaluation can be done with the mean recognition accuracy, which is the sum of true positive and true negative classifications divided by the total number of samples in the evaluation set, or a ROC curve that was already introduced in Section 4.2.

Following some highly recommendable surveys [16, 465, 466], we identify two categories of algorithms for face recognition: holistic and feature based approaches. Starting with holistic approaches, a method called Eigenfaces [485] is proposed in an early work for face images in the VIS spectrum that was adopted in [486] for the LWIR band. The basic idea is to consider the image content in its entirety and project it to a lower dimensional subspace of for a more efficient representation. This projection is done using the Principal Component Analysis (PCA), which is an unsupervised machine learning technique and learns its model for the subspace projection purely data driven. Further information about the PCA is provided in [487]. An average face image calculated from a set of training images is used to determine the eigenvectors with highest eigenvalues that then are assumed to best represent a face space approximation [466]. Within this subspace, each face is given by a set of weights that can be compared to other faces inside a database using for example the nearest neighbor method based on Euclidean distance [485].

Variation in illumination, however, strongly affects the performance of PCA-based face recognition performance. In order to overcome these limitations, supervised learning can be used for dimensionality reduction. The Linear Discriminant Analysis (LDA) that is also known as Fisherfaces or the Independent Component Analysis (ICA) are popular methods that can significantly outperform PCA based approaches [488]. Finally, dimensionality reduction can be performed in the frequency domain, too. The face image can be transformed from the spatial to the frequency domain using the Discrete Cosine Transform (DCT). The image content is then given by DCT coefficients that represent the different frequencies within the image. Assuming that high frequencies originate from image noise, the lower frequencies can be considered as meaningful features and hence can be evaluated by an SVM to distinguish between faces of different individuals [489].

Feature-based approaches aim at extracting (usually local) features, concatenating or recombining them to a feature vector for representation, and finally comparing such vectors with existing or learned metrics. Local features can be for example local appearance patterns such as edges, small shapes, facial landmarks, or face elements like eyes, nose, or mouth, as well as the vascular network or the blood perfusion of the face, which is obviously done for thermal IR images only. Usually, features are chosen that implicitly are or explicitly can be made invariant to certain effects like pose change, illumination, or temperature differences. This is one of the main reasons why feature-based methods usually show superior performance in face recognition compared to holistic approaches. Local appearance patterns are more commonly extracted in the NIR spectrum using geometric distances of facial landmarks, Local Binary Patterns (LBP), or wavelet transform [468, 490, 491], respectively. For thermal IR images originating from MWIR or LWIR cameras, correlation filters [492], wavelet transform [493], or curvelet transform [494] can be applied. Typical metrics used to compare feature vectors are Euclidean distance or data-driven metric learning, which is the most promising and thus most popular approach. The basic idea of metric learning is to determine a distance metric (often a matrix), that maximizes the distance between vectors of different individuals while minimizing the distance between vectors of the same individual at the same time. Kostinger [495] provides a comprehensive introduction to metric learning in his dissertation for further reading. Finally, methods using facial vascular networks or blood perfusion work slightly different and are thus mentioned not in the context of feature extraction and distance metrics. In both approaches, a foreground-background segmentation is performed, where either blood vessels or image regions of high blood perfusion are considered as foreground and thus are emphasized. For the analysis of vascular networks, morphological filters, binarization, and skeletization are suggested [496] followed by the evaluation of so-called thermal minutia points, which is a technique adopted from fingerprint recognition. In a more recent work [479], a soft representation instead of binarization was used and an Active Appearance Model (AAM) was introduced to improve scale and pose invariance. The analysis of blood perfusion as discussed in [16] is usually achieved by a mathematical model that is used to generate a blood perfusion image from an original segmented thermogram that only contains the face of an individual with emphasized blood perfusion regions. Such models are proposed for example in [497] and the resulting blood perfusion images can be classified using neural networks or further feature extraction [498]. Konuk [454] demonstrates that the fusion of vascular network and blood perfusion features can even improve the performance of face recognition compared to the individual approaches.

The best performance within the current state-of-the-art in face recognition that in some cases even reaches the level of human perception is achieved using deep learning techniques in the VIS spectrum [462, 499]. A popular approach is to utilize metric learning for DCNNs by introducing appropriate loss functions to be minimized during training such as contrastive loss [500] or triplet loss [501]. In this way, the aforementioned holistic or feature based approaches can be outperformed by large margin. However, while it was possible to mirror methods developed for the VIS spectrum to the IR spectrum for those approaches, things are different when considering deep learning. The reason is that the training process for deep learning is strongly dependent on sufficient amount of data. State-of-the-art approaches [502] in the VIS domain use about 5 million images taken from more than 75,000 classes to train their DCNNs. This is possible nowadays, as several large VIS datasets such as MegaFace (MF) [484] or MS-Celeb-1M [503] have been published within the last years. With such huge amount of data, invariances to illumination, pose, facial expressions, or even aging of subjects can be learned implicitly and purely data driven during the training stage, which makes deep learning such a powerful approach. Even missing data can be effectively simulated such as additional poses using GANs as demonstrated by [504] or occluded face regions using a deep convolutional encoder-decoder [505]. Since no IR datasets of comparable extend like MF or MS-Celeb-1M exist at this time, Bihn [483] states that deep learning can be applied without any constraints in the VIS spectrum only up to now. One attempt to narrow this data gap between VIS and IR is given in [506], where deep learning is applied in order to hallucinate VIS images from NIR images. Then, a DCNN can be applied that was pre-trained on VIS images only.

In addition to pure VIS, NIR, or LWIR-based face recognition, multi-spectral, or multi-modal data fusion can be a promising approach to increase the robustness. This means that cross-spectral synergies can be utilized to reduce for example the effects of varying illumination or increase inter-subject discrimination [507]. Some authors [508–510] analyze the benefit of fusion VIS and NIR image, while other authors [511, 512] propose fusion approaches for VIS and LWIR. For further reading about face recognition in the IR spectrum, the already mentioned surveys [16, 465, 466] are recommended. The survey of Ghiass et al. [16] is especially worth reading due to its thoroughness and comprehensibility.

Cross-spectral approaches in the face recognition domain are often motivated by the vulnerability of VIS spectrum recognition systems to spoofing attacks. Spoofing is the act of masquerading as a valid user by falsifying data to gain an illegitimate access. Sometime, just by displaying printed photos or replaying recorded videos on mobile devices is enough to get access using biometrics applications. The weakness of deep learning-based face detectors to adversarial

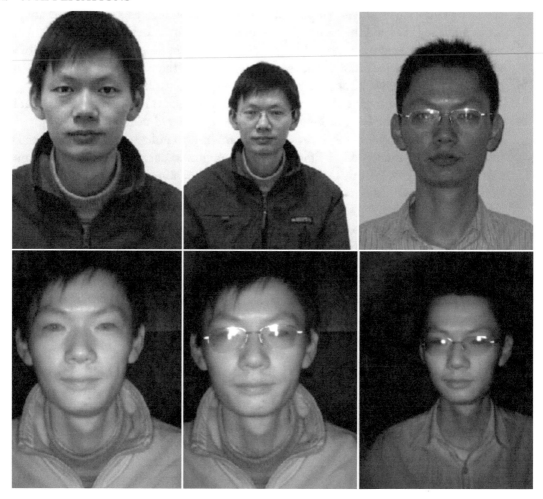

Figure 5.6: Sample images from the CASIA NIR-VIS 2.0 dataset [474]: VIS images (top) and related NIR images (bottom).

attacks was presented in [513] for instance. The authors investigate the security of the well-known cascade CNN face detection system (MTCNN) and propose an easily reproducible and robust way to attack it both in a digital domain as well as in the real world. Having in mind this weakness, different deep learning-based heterogeneous face recognition approaches were proposed in recent years [514–516] together with datasets and benchmarks commonly used for evaluation (see Table 5.1). Figure 5.6 presents some illustrations from one of these datasets. In [516], a coupled auto-associative neural network was introduced to learn the target-to-source image representation for heterogeneous face recognition. The architecture is a kind of two neural networks with hidden units forced to be as similar as possible. The effectiveness of the proposed model is evaluated by using several heterogeneous face recognition databases—NIR-VIS, MWIR-VIS, LWIR-VIS, and sketch-VIS. A similar coupled scheme was proposed in [514], but in this case a Coupled Generative Adversarial Network (CpGAN) is proposed to address the problem of matching non-visible facial imagery with a gallery of faces in the VIS spectrum. Like in the previous case the architecture consists of two networks, one dedicated to the VIS spectrum image and the other to non-VIS spectrum image. Finally, a domain adaptation framework was proposed [515] in that combines a feature mapping sub-network with existing deep feature models (e.g., VGG-16 or ResNet-50). The manuscript includes a study on viability of challenging tasks, such as non-frontal thermal-to-visible face recognition.

## 5.4    EMBEDDED VISION FOR MOVING PLATFORMS

Writing about driver assistance and autonomous vehicles can easily fill books [517, 518]. As a result, we refrain from digging too deep into this topic here. Instead, we referred to these applications multiple times within the related sections of Chapter 4 for example. So, while discussing driver assistance and autonomous driving only briefly here, we focus on other moving platforms such as UAVs and Unmanned Ground Vehicles (UGVs) that utilize IR imagery for various different applications such as smart farming or agriculture. The term *embedded* denotes image and video processing algorithms that run on miniaturized Systems on a Chip (SoCs), which usually can perform computer vision tasks highly efficient with low power consumption and low thermal emission while meeting real-time requirements at the same time. In this context, one could consider a standard smartphone as a moving platform with embedded vision, too. But we think of more practical applications instead of entertainment and hence do not discuss smartphone related applications here.

In recent years, motivated by the reduction in price and size, different embedded vision applications for moving platforms have been developed by using NIR imaging. We can find on-board NIR-based applications for autonomous vehicles and driver assistance, UAV related applications, robotics agriculture, or image enhancement in the mobile devices. This section presents just a few applications of embedded NIR acquisition systems as mentioned above. Remote sensing is skipped since it is out of the scope of this book.

In road traffic scenarios we can find NIR based applications for both driver assistance and autonomous driving [243]. These applications need to face challenging uncontrolled outdoor scenarios (e.g., poor lighting conditions or scene with camouflaged objects due to the surface color or texture), hence other passive and cheap sensors that complement VIS spectrum on-board cameras are required. Looking at the literature there is a large number of publications on NIR image based driving applications. Actually, some of them intended for object detection (e.g., pedestrian, vehicles) have already been reviewed in Section 4.2. There are also some applications for visual odometry that use NIR imagery along with other imaging sensors [519]. Even Simultaneous Localization And Mapping (SLAM) problems can be supported by IR imagery:

Figure 5.7: On-board vision systems: electric vehicle from the Computer Vision Center (CVC) in Barcelona, Spain with VIS and LWIR cameras on top [136] (left), UAV for smart farming applications [529] (center), and *VineScout* autonomous robot with NIR vision system for applications in agriculture [532] (right).

SWIR cameras are well-known for their ability to mitigate haze. Hence, they are well-suited for applications in challenging environments [520]. Additionally, like in some of the applications presented above, there are also some cross-spectral approaches, where robust solutions have been proposed by utilizing the information from two or more spectral bands. One of the pioneering work on the usage of combined information toward a robust pedestrian detection system has been presented in [157]. In this work the authors evaluate color-, IR-, and multimodal-stereo approaches for pedestrian detection by designing a four-camera sensor suite consisting of two RGB and two IR cameras. From the acquisition system different combinations were evaluated (monocular and stereo information) reaching the best performance with a trifocal setup consisting of a stereo camera in the VIS spectrum coupled with an IR camera. The image registration through the different modalities is performed at an object detection level, i.e., similar pedestrians detected across the cameras are used as features for image alignment. In this way, image registration for the entire image at a pixel level is avoided, which can be a benefit as cross-spectral image registration is challenging (see Section 3.1). Since that seminal work, several contributions to the pedestrian detection task in cross-spectral domains were presented for driver assistance applications. In recent years, most of the contributions are deep learning-based approaches, where a DCNN is trained to exploit information from two spectral bands, which usually is either NIR or LWIR together with VIS for detecting pedestrians or vehicles. An interesting approach is presented in [307], where a DCNN uses LWIR-VIS image pairs to learn related LWIR features for a given VIS image. Then, this DCNN is applied to pure VIS images and hallucinates the LWIR features in order to improve the detection performance under difficult illumination conditions. Compared with traditional pedestrian detection, cross-spectral pedestrian detection suffers from modality imbalance problems as well as for image misalignment issues. Regarding imbalance problems, in [312] a novel DCNN architecture (MB-Net: Modality Balance Network) is proposed. It facilitates the optimization process in a much more flexible and balanced way. In general, cross-spectral architectures are trained in a supervised way, where a pair of cross-spectral images is provided during training process. These approaches are again affected by misalignment in real-world scenarios [208]. To overcome this problem [521] proposes a novel learning framework for cross-spectral pedestrian detection in an unpaired setting. The proposed framework is based on an adversarial learning scheme that merge features from color and thermal IR images. A specific section on multi-spectral person detection is provided in Section 4.2.

In addition to ground-based vehicle applications, on-board infrared cameras are also used for applications of UAVs. Addabbo et al. [522] for instance propose a low-cost system for photovoltaic plant inspection. The system is based on a UAV equipped with a thermal camera to detect thermal anomalies on panels that can affect their functionality and performance. On-board thermal IR cameras have been used also in applications devoted to civil safety: UAVs equipped with such cameras can be suitable platforms for speeding up search and rescue operations [523] or the detection of forest fires [524, 525]. The reason is that persons trapped in water or in a forest usually have a distinct thermal IR signature compared to the background and thus can be detected much faster compared to VIS imagery. The same property applies to fire for obvious reasons. We can also find applications for cultural heritage conservation. For instance, [526] present details of the integration of a thermal IR camera and a UAV to detect rupestrian sites to be preserved. Also based on the ground floor observation from UAVs, [527] present a thermal IR imaging system to detect structural damage of buildings and cracks in external walls after an earthquake. This loss assessment system can be also used in emergency rescue. Finally, in recent years, an increasing number of contributions have been proposed for the agriculture field. One of them is the estimation of the Normalized Difference Vegetation Index (NDVI) from UAVs; the NDVI is obtained as the ratio between information from the VIS and the NIR spectral bands and it is often used to monitor drought, to forecast agricultural production, and to assist in forecasting fire zones [528, 529]. The vegetation index is also used to estimate the water consumption of crops and predict dry biomass and crop yield [530]. Furthermore, the SWIR band can effectively support vegetation monitoring since the chlorophyll content of plants can be measured [531]. Agriculture applications have been using IR imaging on-board not only on UAV systems but also on autonomous UGVs [532]. In this case, infrared imaging is used mainly for detection and classification tasks.

As already mentioned, this section does not pretend to be an exhaustive list of applications from state-of-the-art embedded vision systems for moving platforms but rather an illustration of some of the different recent contributions.

CHAPTER 6

# Summary and Outlook

In this book, an overview was given of the current state-of-the-art in computer vision and machine learning based on IR imagery. Four topics that each provide a sufficient foundation of related literature were discussed in more detail: (1) IR image and video enhancement; (2) cross-spectral image processing; (3) detection, classification, and tracking; and (4) applications based on IR imagery. Image enhancement was presented from the imaging point of view, where noise and other imaging artifacts are reduced, and from the long-range observation point of view, where atmospheric effects are mitigated and the limited spatial image resolution is magnified. A human operator, who analyzes the scene content, can benefit from such enhancement techniques, but also algorithms that do not implicitly handle impaired image quality. Cross-spectral image processing is an interesting topic since modern sensor suites often come with a combination of cameras and other sensors that can be smartly combined to complement each other. In contrast to multi-spectral computer vision, where information is fused and processed together, here we aimed at describing approaches, where one spectral band guides or aids the other band and vice versa. Detection, classification, and tracking in IR imagery aim at extracting higher-level information that can be used for the automation of various tasks in surveillance, automotive, and robotics applications. Hence, a separate chapter was dedicated to applications showing how the algorithms and methods described before can be utilized specifically.

For each topic, typical properties, scientific challenges as well as popular benchmarks, dataset, and evaluation measures were presented. Machine learning plays a key role in computer vision nowadays and was thus particularly discussed across all the topics ranging from traditional statistical methods to modern deep learning techniques. Although nearly all computer vision challenges originate from VIS imagery, great attention was paid to compare the differences and similarities of IR imagery enhancement and exploitation in the VIS and the different IR spectra. VIS, NIR, and SWIR cameras capture reflection light and need active illumination. Thermal MWIR and LWIR cameras are sensitive to emitted infrared radiation and do not need any illumination. In the literature, NIR and thermal IR are the most widely used IR sub-bands. While the NIR spectrum is often used as an extension of VIS imagery to achieve higher robustness against illumination changes, the thermal IR spectra MWIR and LWIR are rather used as a complementing source of information especially in case of insufficient illumination. As several authors state, an observed scene has a rather similar appearance in VIS and NIR since these spectral bands are neighbors in the electromagnetic spectrum. Instead, scenes and objects appear much less textured in thermal IR images due to the rather smooth temperature profile of objects. Cross- and multi-spectral computer vision uses at least two different spectral bands in order to achieve higher robustness to illumination or temperature changes. Especially combined VIS and thermal IR have proven to provide powerful synergies in different tasks such as person detection.

Having a closer look at the related applications, we can see that a recommendation for certain sensors, sensor combinations, or spectral bands is highly dependent not only on the application itself but also on the application's environment. As we recall Chapter 2 on IR image and video enhancement, statistics on existing literature and datasets (see Tables 4.1 and 4.2) show that for outdoor scenarios and longer-range imaging such as automotive or surveillance, a thermal IR camera in addition to a VIS camera seems to be most beneficial, while NIR or SWIR cameras are favorable for applications that need rather short-range sensing such as biometrics. But why is this the case? We discussed earlier that weak illumination is one of the main issues for VIS cameras in outdoor scenarios—especially for autonomous systems that need to be operational 24/7. Thermal IR cameras can compensate for this drawback as they measure temperature differences. As in most outdoor applications we aim at detecting man-made objects such as humans or vehicles, we usually can assume that there is a temperature difference between these man-made objects and the surrounding background. Hence, we can use thermal IR cameras to detect potential salience in the scene originating from such objects. However, scenes in the MWIR or LWIR spectral band are usually much less textured compared to the VIS spectrum. Since texture information is crucial for certain computer vision tasks such as object classification or tracking, we still benefit from the additional VIS camera in such scenarios even if sufficient illumination is not always guaranteed. For instance, all papers that evaluate person detection on the KAIST Multispectral Pedestrian Benchmark [63] show that the best detection performance is achieved when both the VIS and the LWIR spectral band are considered simultaneously. Even LWIR alone outperforms pure VIS but this depends on the data, of course: the more data with weakly illuminated scenes makes up the used dataset, the better pure LWIR based detection approaches perform. However, this recommendation strongly considers the tradeoff of performance and price. Cooled thermal IR cameras are still very costly but they can provide both a scene sensed invariant to illumination and rich textures for generating high quality appearance features. On the other hand, we have biometrics related applications such as face recognition or iris scanning. The statistics of the available literature and datasets (see Table 5.1) show that here the NIR and the SWIR spectral bands are much more popular. Again, this can be explained with the application's environment: we sense in a more collaborative environment and in shorter range. Salience becomes less important but fine-grained texture information is crucial that especially is independent of certain artifacts such as shadows. This means, shadows in the VIS spectrum can be ignored when using cameras in the NIR or the SWIR spectrum, which actively illuminate the scene in a wave-length the human cannot see but that can remove shadows before the image is captured. Furthermore, thermal IR cameras cannot look through plain glass, which is a disadvantage if the human to be verified wears glasses (see Fig. 5.5). Finally, another important aspect is that cameras sensitive to VIS, NIR, or SWIR are less sensitive to the human condition: the same person at regular temperature or sweating can have a significantly different appearance in the thermal IR spectral bands [16]. Of course, there are applications, in which these findings do not apply like for example fever detection, where we primarily care about the person's temperature but not the identity.

There are more interesting computer vision tasks that were not covered in this book. We intentionally skipped any tasks related to medical imaging or visual inspection as those use more specialized approaches of IR image processing that we consider individual fields of research with an already active community [9, 533, 534]. Among the tasks that we would have liked to cover is for example fine-grained image classification with the challenge to distinguish between hundreds or even thousands of different object classes. Here we obviously lack of commonly and publicly available IR data as there is no *IR ImageNet* or *IR COCO* dataset up to now. New larger-scale datasets for DCNN training and algorithm evaluation in certain tasks appear regularly [145, 349], but still they lack behind their counterparts in the VIS spectrum by orders of magnitudes regarding the size and the covered scenarios. In the meantime, it can be an alternative to utilize synthetic IR data for machine learning since novel deep learning techniques proved to benefit from using such data when training DCNNs. GANs are modern and powerful tools to generate synthetic data of high quality [374]. Due to the decreasing costs and hence the growing spread of IR cameras utilized not only for military but also for surveillance, automotive, and robotics applications, IR imagery enhancement and exploitation is a vital field of research with a still growing community.

What remains is that we are definitely not done at this time. IR sensors have not yet found their way into our everyday lives including for instance consumer electronics or standard sensor suites for large-scale applications such as autonomous driving. The balance between sensor price and imaging quality is still not satisfactory: while relatively inexpensive uncooled thermal IR sensors (microbolometers) cannot always achieve high image quality especially under adverse environmental conditions, cooled thermal IR cameras can produce images of highest quality but they are still expensive to purchase and maintain. As a result, even video surveillance, which is an application that strongly benefits from using thermal IR cameras, is still preferably done with VIS cameras in order to be price efficient. The situation is even worse for SWIR imaging devices that have not yet profited from a scaling effect in production. Nevertheless, the potential benefit of using such imaging devices stand-alone or integrating it as another modality to an existing sensor suite is huge as we discovered in this book. As soon as IR sensors have established themselves in large-scale mass applications, of which autonomous driving seems to be the most promising one at this time, the way may be paved for many more applications in biometrics, robotics, and video surveillance.

# Bibliography

[1] D. W. Hansen and R. Hammoud, An improved likelihood model for eye tracking, *Computer Vision and Image Understanding (CVIU)*, 106(2–3):220–230, 2007. DOI: 10.1016/j.cviu.2006.06.012. 2, 66

[2] M. Livingstone and D. H. Hubel, *Vision and Art: The Biology of Seeing*, N. Abrams Inc., 2008. 2

[3] W. R. McCluney, *Introduction to Radiometry and Photometry*, Artech House, 2014. 2

[4] D. A. Forsyth and J. Ponce, *Computer Vision: A Modern Approach*, Prentice Hall, 2002. 2

[5] R. Szeliski, *Computer Vision: Algorithms and Applications*, Springer, 2010. 2

[6] R. Gade and T. Moeslund, Thermal cameras and applications: A survey, *Machine Vision and Applications*, 25(1):245–262, 2014. DOI: 10.1007/s00138-013-0570-5. 2, 6, 19

[7] A. Berg, Detection and tracking in thermal infrared imagery, Licentiate thesis, Linköping University, Linköping, Sweden, 2016. DOI: 10.3384/lic.diva-126955. 3, 6, 40

[8] Santa Barbara Research Center, *Data Source*, 2018. 4

[9] M. Vollmer and K.-P. Möllmann, *Infrared Thermal Imaging: Fundamentals, Research and Applications*, Wiley, 2010. DOI: 10.1002/9783527630868. 3, 15, 79

[10] W. G. Rees, *Physical Principles of Remote Sensing*, Cambridge University Press, 2001. DOI: 10.1017/cbo9780511812903. 3

[11] A. Daniels, *Field Guide to Infrared Systems*, Society for Optical Engineering, Bellingham, 2007. DOI: 10.1117/3.684619. 3

[12] B. B. Turgut, Radiometry-based range prediction for mid- and long-wave infrared imaging systems, Dissertation, Middle East Technical University, Turkey, 2018. 3

[13] D. Olmeda, C. Premebida, U. Nunes, J. M. Armingol, and A. de la Escalera, Pedestrian classification and detection in far infrared images, *Integrated Computer-Aided Engineering*, 20:347–360, 2013. DOI: 10.3233/ICA-130441. 4, 42, 43

[14] Y. Socarras, S. Ramos, D. Vazquez, A. Lopez, and T. Gevers, Adapting pedestrian detection from synthetic to far infrared images, *IEEE ICCV Workshops*, 2013. 4, 42, 43

[15] T. Karasawa, K. Watanabe, Q. Ha, A. Tejero-De-Pablos, U. Yoshitaka, and T. Harada, Multispectral object detection for autonomous vehicles, *ACMMM Workshops*, 2017. 4, 5, 6, 43, 64, 65

[16] R. S. Ghiass, O. Arandjelovic, A. Bendada, and X. Maldague, Infrared face recognition: A comprehensive review of methodologies and databases, *Pattern Recognition*, 47(9):2807–2824, 2014. DOI: 10.1016/j.patcog.2014.03.015. 4, 68, 69, 70, 71, 79

[17] C. A. Aguilera, F. J. Aguilera, A. D. Sappa, C. Aguilera, and R. Toledo, Learning cross-spectral similarity measures with deep convolutional neural networks, *IEEE CVPR Workshops*, 2016. DOI: 10.1109/cvprw.2016.40. 4, 5, 27

[18] S. Hu, N. Short, B. S. Riggan, M. Chasse, and M. S. Sarfraz, Heterogeneous face recognition: Recent advances in infrared-to-visible matching, *IEEE International Conference on Automatic Face and Gesture Recognition*, 2017. DOI: 10.1109/fg.2017.126. 4

[19] S. Kim, W.-J. Song, and S.-H. Kim, Infrared variation optimized deep convolutional neural network for robust automatic ground target recognition, *IEEE CVPR Workshops*, 2017. DOI: 10.1109/cvprw.2017.30. 4, 62

[20] D. Rüfenacht, C. Fredembach, and S. Süsstrunk, Automatic and accurate shadow detection using near-infrared information, *IEEE Transactions on Pattern Analysis and Machine Intelligence*, 36(8):1672–1678, 2014. DOI: 10.1109/tpami.2013.229. 5

[21] L. Schaul, C. Fredembach, and S. Süsstrunk, Color image dehazing using the near-infrared, *IEEE International Conference on Image Processing (ICIP)*, 2009. DOI: 10.1109/icip.2009.5413700. 5, 32

[22] P. Pinggera, T. Breckon, and H. Bischof, On cross-spectral stereo matching using dense gradient features, *British Machine Vision Conference (BMVC)*, 2012. DOI: 10.5244/c.26.103. 6, 25

[23] B. Li, W. Ren, D. Fu, D. Tao, D. Feng, W. Zeng, and Z. Wang, Benchmarking single-image dehazing and beyond, *IEEE Transactions on Image Processing*, 28(1):492–505, 2019. DOI: 10.1109/TIP.2018.2867951. 9, 16

[24] O. Oreifej, X. Li, and M. Shah, Simultaneous video stabilization and moving object detection in turbulence, *IEEE Transactions on Pattern Analysis and Machine Intelligence*, 35(2):450–462, 2013. DOI: 10.1109/tpami.2012.97. 9, 17, 18

[25] S. Milyaev and I. Laptev, Towards reliable object detection in noisy images, *Pattern Recognition and Image Analysis*, 27:713–722, 2017. DOI: 10.1134/s1054661817040149. 9

[26] E. Simoncelli and B. Olshausen, Natural image statistics and neural representation, *Annual Review of Neuroscience*, 24:1193–1216, 2001. DOI: 10.1146/annurev.neuro.24.1.1193. 9

[27] H. Sheikh, M. Sabir, and A. Bovik, A statistical evaluation of recent full reference image quality assessment algorithms, *IEEE Transactions on Image Processing*, 15(11):3440–3451, 2006. DOI: 10.1109/tip.2006.881959. 9

[28] L. Zhang, L. Zhang, X. Mou, and D. Zhang, A comprehensive evaluation of full reference image quality assessment algorithms, *IEEE ICIP*, 2012. DOI: 10.1109/icip.2012.6467150. 10

[29] Z. Wang, A. Bovik, H. Sheikh, and E. Simoncelli, Image quality assessment: From error visibility to structural similarity, *IEEE Transactions on Image Processing*, 13(4):600–612, 2004. DOI: 10.1109/tip.2003.819861. 10

[30] H. Sheikh and A. Bovik, Image information and visual quality, *IEEE Transactions on Image Processing*, 15(2):430–444, 2006. DOI: 10.1109/tip.2005.859378. 10

[31] A. Mittal, A. Moorthy, and A. Bovik, No-reference image quality assessment in the spatial domain, *IEEE Transactions on Image Processing*, 21(12):4695–4708, 2012. DOI: 10.1109/tip.2012.2214050. 10

[32] A. Mittal, R. Soundararajan, and A. Bovik, Making a completely blind image quality analyzer, *IEEE Signal Processing Letters*, 22(3):209–212, 2013. DOI: 10.1109/lsp.2012.2227726. 10

[33] R. Zhang, P. Isola, A. Efros, E. Shechtman, and O. Wang, The unreasonable effectiveness of deep features as a perceptual metric, *IEEE CVPR*, 2018. DOI: 10.1109/cvpr.2018.00068. 10

[34] Z. Tu, Y. Wang, N. Birkbeck, B. Adsumilli, and A. C. Bovik, UGC-VQA: Benchmarking blind video quality assessment for user generated content, *IEEE Transactions on Image Processing*, 30:4449–4464, 2021. DOI: 10.1109/tip.2021.3072221. 10

[35] T. Goodall, A. Bovik, and N. Paulter, Tasking on natural statistics of infrared images, *IEEE Transactions on Image Processing*, 25(1):65–79, 2016. DOI: 10.1109/tip.2015.2496289. 10

[36] Y. Tendero, S. Landeau, and J. Gilles, Non-uniformity correction of infrared images by midway equalization, *Image Processing On Line (IPOL)*, 2:134–146, 2012. DOI: 10.5201/ipol.2012.glmt-mire. 10, 12

[37] H. Leng, Z. Zhou, W. Liu, B. Yi, Q. Xie, D. Wu, and J. Cao, New scene-based adaptive bad pixel detection algorithm for IRFPA, *Proc. SPIE*, 8907, 2013. DOI: 10.1117/12.2033162. 10

[38] H. Luo, L. Xu, B. Hui, and Z. Chang, Tone mapping infrared images using conditional filtering-based multi-scale retinex, *Proc. SPIE*, 9675, 2015. DOI: 10.1117/12.2202187. 10

[39] S. Dodge and L. Karam, Understanding how image quality affects deep neural networks, *International Conference on Quality of Multimedia Experience (QoMEX)*, 2016. DOI: 10.1109/qomex.2016.7498955. 10

[40] C. Boncelet, Image noise models, *The Essential Guide to Image Processing*, Springer, pages 143–167, 2009. DOI: 10.1016/B978-0-12-374457-9.00007-X. 11

[41] M. Bertalmio (Ed.), *Denoising of Photographic Images and Video*, Springer, 2018. DOI: 10.1007/978-3-319-96029-6. 11

[42] S. Gu and R. Timofte, A brief review of image denoising algorithms and beyond, *Inpainting and Denoising Challenges*, pages 1–21, Springer, 2019. DOI: 10.1007/978-3-030-25614-2_1. 11

[43] A. Abdelhamed et al., NTIRE 2020 challenge on real image denoising: Dataset, methods and results, *IEEE CVPR Workshops*, 2020. DOI: 10.1109/cvprw50498.2020.00256. 11

[44] M. Maggioni, G. Boracchi, A. Foi, and K. Egiazarian, Video denoising, deblocking, and enhancement through separable 4D nonlocal spatiotemporal transforms, *IEEE Transactions on Image Processing*, 21(9):3952–3966, 2012. DOI: 10.1109/tip.2012.2199324. 11

[45] M. Tassano, J. Delon, and T. Veit, FastDVDnet: Towards real-time deep video denoising without flow estimation, *IEEE CVPR*, 2020. DOI: 10.1109/cvpr42600.2020.00143. 11

[46] J. Weickert, *Anisotropic Diffusion in Image Processing*, B. G. Teubner Stuttgart, 1998. DOI: 10.1007/978-3-7091-6586-7_13. 11

[47] S. Paris, P. Kornprobst, J. Tumblin, and F. Durand, Bilateral filtering: Theory and applications, *Foundations and Trends in Computer Graphics and Vision*, 4(1):1–73, 2009. DOI: 10.1561/0600000020. 11

[48] J. Lehtinen, J. Munkberg, J. Hasselgren, S. Laine, T. Karras, M. Aittala, and T. Aila, Noise2Noise: Learning image restoration without clean data, *International Conference on Machine Learning (ICML)*, 2018. 11

[49] T. Ehret, A. Davy, and J. Morel, Model-blind video denoising via frame-to-frame training, *IEEE CVPR*, 2019. DOI: 10.1109/cvpr.2019.01163. 11

[50] N. Moran, D. Schmidt, Y. Zhong, and P. Coady, Noisier2Noise: Learning to denoise from unpaired noisy data, *IEEE CVPR*, 2020. DOI: 10.1109/cvpr42600.2020.01208. 11

[51] L. Jing and Y. Tian, Self-supervised visual feature learning with deep neural networks: A survey, *IEEE Transactions on Pattern Analysis and Machine Intelligence*, Early Access, 2020. DOI: 10.1109/tpami.2020.2992393. 11

[52] H. V. Kennedy, Modeling noise in thermal imaging systems, *Proc. SPIE*, 1969, 1993. DOI: 10.1117/12.154739. 11

[53] A. Rogalski, *Infrared Detectors*, CRC Press, 2011. DOI: 10.1201/b10319. 11

[54] S. Budzan and R. Wyzgolik, Noise reduction in thermal images, *International Conference on Computer Vision and Graphics (ICCVG)*, 2014. DOI: 10.1007/978-3-319-11331-9_15. 11

[55] B. Zhou, S. Wang, Y. Ma, X. Mei, B. Li, H. Li, and F. Fan, An IR image impulse noise suppression algorithm based on fuzzy logic, *Infrared Physics and Technology*, 60:346–358, 2013. DOI: 10.1016/j.infrared.2013.06.005. 11

[56] Y. Binbin, An improved infrared image processing method based on adaptive threshold denoising, *EURASIP Journal on Image and Video Processing*, 5, 2019. DOI: 10.1186/s13640-018-0401-8. 12

[57] B. Dee-Noor, A. Stern, Y. Yitzhaky, and N. Kopeika, Infrared image denoising by non-local means filtering, *Proc. SPIE*, 8399, 2012. DOI: 10.1117/12.919979. 12

[58] Z. Liu, C. Sun, X. Bai, and F. Zhou, Infrared ship target image smoothing based on adaptive mean shift, *Digital Image Computing: Techniques and Applications*, 2014. DOI: 10.1109/dicta.2014.7008113. 12

[59] P. Meza, C. San Martin, E. Vera, and S. Torres, A quantitative evaluation of fixed-pattern noise reduction methods in imaging systems, *Iberoamerican Congress on Pattern Recognition (CIARP)*, 2010. DOI: 10.1007/978-3-642-16687-7_40. 12

[60] M. Guan, R. Lai, A. Xiong, Z. Liu, and L. Gu, Fixed pattern noise reduction for infrared images based on cascade residual attention CNN, *Elsevier Neurocomputing*, 377:301–313, 2014. DOI: 10.1016/j.neucom.2019.10.054. 12

[61] Y. Cao, Z. He, J. Yang, Y. Cao, and M. Ying Yang, Spatially adaptive column fixed-pattern noise correction in infrared imaging system using 1D horizontal differential statistics, *IEEE Photonics Journal*, 9(5), 2017. DOI: 10.1109/jphot.2017.2752000. 12

[62] M. Maggioni, E. Sanchez-Monge, and A. Foi, Joint removal of random and fixed-pattern noise through spatiotemporal video filtering, *IEEE Transactions on Image Processing*, 23(10):4282–4296, 2014. DOI: 10.1109/tip.2014.2345261. 12

[63] S. Hwang, J. Park, N. Kim, Y. Choi, and I. S. Kweon, Multispectral pedestrian detection: Benchmark dataset and baseline, *IEEE CVPR*, 2015. DOI: 10.1109/cvpr.2015.7298706. 12, 13, 24, 29, 40, 43, 45, 46, 56, 78

[64] R. C. Gonzalez and R. E. Woods, *Digital Image Processing*, Prentice Hall International, 2008. DOI: 10.2307/1574313. 13

[65] L. Yu, H. Su, and C. Jung, Joint enhancement and denoising of low light images via JND transform, *IEEE International Conference on Acoustics, Speech and Signal Processing (ICASSP)*, 2020. DOI: 10.1109/icassp40776.2020.9053027. 13

[66] R. Highnam and M. Brady, Model-based image enhancement of far infrared images, *IEEE Transactions on Pattern Analysis and Machine Intelligence*, 19(4):410–415, 1997. DOI: 10.1109/34.588029. 13

[67] C.-L. Lin, An approach to adaptive infrared image enhancement for long-range surveillance, *Infrared Physics and Technology*, 54(2):84–91, 2011. DOI: 10.1016/j.infrared.2011.01.001. 14

[68] M. Wan, G. Gu, W. Qian, K. Ren, Q. Chen, and X. Maldague, Infrared image enhancement using adaptive histogram partition and brightness correction, *MDPI Remote Sensing*, 10(5), 2018. DOI: 10.3390/rs10050682. 14

[69] J. Roman, J. Noguera, H. Legal-Ayala, D. Pinto-Roa, S. Gomez-Guerrero, and M. Garcia Torres, Entropy and contrast enhancement of infrared thermal images using the multiscale top-hat transform, *MDPI Entropy*, 21(3), 2019. DOI: 10.3390/e21030244. 14

[70] C. Liu, X. Sui, X. Kuang, Y. Liu, G. Gu, and Q. Chen, Adaptive contrast enhancement for infrared images based on the neighborhood conditional histogram, *MDPI Remote Sensing*, 11(11), 2019. DOI: 10.3390/rs11111381. 14

[71] C. Liu, X. Sui, X. Kuang, Y. Liu, G. Gu, and Q. Chen, Optimized contrast enhancement for infrared images based on global and local histogram specification, *MDPI Remote Sensing*, 11(7), 2019. DOI: 10.3390/rs11070849. 14, 52

[72] P. Bhattacharya, J. Riechen, and U. Zölzer, Infrared image enhancement in maritime environment with convolutional neural networks, *International Conference on Computer Vision Theory and Application*, 2018. DOI: 10.5220/0006618700370046. 14

[73] R. Rivadeneira, A. Sappa, and B. Vintimilla, Thermal image super-resolution: A novel architecture and dataset, *International Conference on Computer Vision Theory and Application (VISAPP)*, 2020. DOI: 10.5220/0009173601110119. 14, 20, 21

[74] J. Howell, R. Siegel, and M. Menguc, *Thermal Radiation Heat Transfer*, Taylor & Francis Inc., 2015. DOI: 10.1201/b18835. 14

[75] F. Smith (Ed.), *Atmospheric Propagation of Radiation (The Infrared and Electro-Optical Systems Handbook, Volume 2)*, Infrared Info. Analysis Ctr & SPIE Optical Engineering Press, 1993. 14

[76] J. Lang, Y. Wang, X. Xiao, X. Zhuang, S. Wang, J. Liu, and J. Wang, Study on shortwave infrared long-distance imaging performance based on multiband imaging experiments, *SPIE Optical Engineering*, 52(4):1–10, 2013. DOI: 10.1117/1.oe.52.4.045008. 15

[77] M. Bertozzi, R. I. Fedriga, A. Miron, and J.-L. Reverchon, Pedestrian detection in poor visibility conditions: Would SWIR help?, *International Conference on Image Analysis and Processing (ICIAP)*, 2013. DOI: 10.1007/978-3-642-41184-7_24. 15

[78] R. Fattal, Single image dehazing, *ACM Transactions on Graphics*, 27(3), 2008. DOI: 10.1145/1360612.1360671. 15

[79] H. Koschmieder, *Theorie der Horizontalen Sichtweite: Kontrast und Sichtweite*, Keim & Nemnich, 1925. 15

[80] K. He, J. Sun, and X. Tang, Single image haze removal using dark channel prior, *IEEE Transactions on Pattern Analysis and Machine Intelligence*, 33(12):2341–2353, 2011. DOI: 10.1109/tpami.2010.168. 15

[81] D. Berman, T. Treibitz, and S. Avidan, Non-local image dehazing, *IEEE CVPR*, 2016. DOI: 10.1109/cvpr.2016.185. 15

[82] B. Cai, X. Xu, K. Jia, C. Qing, and D. Tao, DehazeNet: An end-to-end system for single image haze removal, *IEEE Transactions on Image Processing*, 25(11):5187–5198, 2016. DOI: 10.1109/tip.2016.2598681. 16

[83] C. O. Ancuti, C. Ancuti, F.-A. Vasluianu, and R. Timofte, NTIRE 2020 challenge on nonhomogeneous dehazing, *IEEE CVPR Workshops*, 2020. DOI: 10.1109/cvprw50498.2020.00253. 16

[84] C. Sakaridis, D. Dai, and L. Van Gool, Semantic foggy scene understanding with synthetic data, *International Journal of Computer Vision (IJCV)*, 126:973–992, 2018. DOI: 10.1007/s11263-018-1072-8. 16

[85] C. O. Ancuti, C. Ancuti, and R. Timofte, NHHAZE: An image dehazing benchmark with nonhomogeneous hazy and haze-free images, *IEEE CVPR Workshops*, 2020. DOI: 10.1109/cvprw50498.2020.00230. 16

[86] E. H. Land, The retinex theory of color vision, *Scientific American*, 237(6):108–128, 1977. DOI: 10.1038/scientificamerican1277-108. 16

[87] J. J. McCann, Retinex at 50: Color theory and spatial algorithms, a review, *SPIE Journal of Electronic Imaging*, 26(3), 2017. DOI: 10.1117/1.jei.26.3.031204. 16

[88] J. Vazquez-Corral, S. W. Zamir, A. Galdran, D. Pardo, and M. Bertalmo, Image processing applications through a variational perceptually-based color correction related to retinex, *Journal of Electronic Imaging*, 2016(6):1–6, 2016. DOI: 10.2352/issn.2470-1173.2016.6.retinex-317. 16

[89] M. Tektonidis and D. Monnin, Color consistency and local contrast enhancement for a mobile image-based change detection system, *Journal of Imaging*, 3(3), 2017. DOI: 10.3390/jimaging3030035. 16

[90] A. Galdran, A. Alvarez-Gila, A. Bria, J. Vazquez-Corral, and M. Bertalmio, On the duality between retinex and image dehazing, *IEEE CVPR*, 2018. DOI: 10.1109/cvpr.2018.00857. 16

[91] B. Xie, F. Guo, and Z. Cai, Improved single image dehazing using dark channel prior and multi-scale retinex, *International Conference on Intelligent System Design and Engineering Application (ISDEA)*, 2010. DOI: 10.1109/isdea.2010.141. 16

[92] A. B. Petro, C. Sbert, J.-M. Morel, Multiscale retinex, *Image Processing on Line (IPOL)*, 4:71–88, 2014. DOI: 10.5201/ipol.2014.107. 16

[93] H. Zhang, X. Liu, Z. Huang, and Y. Ji, Single image dehazing based on fast wavelet transform with weighted image fusion, *IEEE ICIP*, 2014. DOI: 10.1109/icip.2014.7025921. 16

[94] W. Wang, W. Li, Q. Guan, and M. Qi, Multiscale single image dehazing based on adaptive wavelet fusion, *Mathematical Problems in Engineering*, 1:1–14, 2015. DOI: 10.1155/2015/131082. 16

[95] S. Huang, Y. Liu, Y. Wang, Z. Wang, and J. Guo, A new haze removal algorithm for single urban remote sensing image, *IEEE Access*, 8:100870–100889, 2020. DOI: 10.1109/access.2020.2997985. 16

[96] J.-P. Tarel and N. Hautiere, Fast visibility restoration from a single color or gray level image, *IEEE ICCV*, 2009. DOI: 10.1109/iccv.2009.5459251. 16

[97] Q. Tang, J. Yang, X. He, W. Jia, Q. Zhang, and H. Liu, Nighttime image dehazing based on retinex and dark channel prior using Taylor series expansion, *Computer Vision and Image Understanding (CVIU)*, 202:2021. DOI: 10.1016/j.cviu.2020.103086. 16

[98] B. Jiang, W. Zhang, J. Zhao, Y. Ru, M. Liu, X. Ma, X. Chen, and H. Meng, Gray-scale image dehazing guided by scene depth information, *Mathematical Problems in Engineering*, 2016:2016. DOI: 10.1155/2016/7809214. 16

[99] M. Kristo, M. Ivasic-Kos, and M. Pobar, Thermal object detection in difficult weather conditions using YOLO, *IEEE Access*, 8:125459–125476, 2020. DOI: 10.1109/access.2020.3007481. 16

[100] M. Kristo and M. Ivasic-Kos, Thermal imaging dataset for person detection, *International Convention on Information and Communication Technology, Electronics and Microelectronics (MIPRO)*, 2019. DOI: 10.23919/mipro.2019.8757208. 16

[101] M. C. Roggemann and B. M. Welsh, *Imaging Through Turbulence*, CRC Press, 1996. DOI: 10.1201/9780203751282 . 16

[102] R. Nieuwenhuizen and K. Schutte, Deep learning for software-based turbulence mitigation in long-range imaging, *Proc. SPIE*, 11169, 2019. DOI: 10.1117/12.2532603. 17, 18

[103] C. J. Carrano, Mitigating atmospheric effects in high-resolution infrared surveillance imagery with bispectral speckle imaging, *Proc. SPIE*, 6316, 2006. DOI: 10.1117/12.677938. 17, 18

[104] N. Chimitt, Z. Mao, G. Hong, and S. H. Chan, Rethinking atmospheric turbulence mitigation, *ArXiv:1905.07498*, 2019. 17

[105] X. Zhu and P. Milanfar, Removing atmospheric turbulence via space-invariant deconvolution, *IEEE Transactions on Pattern Analysis and Machine Intelligence*, 35(1):157–170, 2013. DOI: 10.1109/tpami.2012.82. 17

[106] R. Hardie and D. LeMaster, On the simulation and mitigation of anisoplanatic optical turbulence for long range imaging, *Proc. SPIE*, 10204, 2017. DOI: 10.1117/12.2264064. 17

[107] N. Anantrasirichai, A. Achim, N. G. Kingsbury, and D. R. Bull, Atmospheric turbulence mitigation using complex wavelet-based fusion, *IEEE Transactions on Image Processing*, 22(6):2398–2408, 2013. DOI: 10.1109/tip.2013.2249078. 17, 18

[108] D. Vint, G. Di Caterina, J. Soraghan, R. Lamb, and D. Humphreys, Analysis of deep learning architectures for turbulence mitigation in long-range imagery, *Proc. SPIE*, 11543, 2020. DOI: 10.1117/12.2573927. 17

[109] N. Anantrasirichai, A. Achim, and D. Bull, Atmospheric turbulence mitigation for sequences with moving objects using recursive image fusion, *IEEE ICIP*, 2018. DOI: 10.1109/icip.2018.8451755. 18

[110] R. Nieuwenhuizen, J. Dijk, and K. Schutte, Dynamic turbulence mitigation for long-range imaging in the presence of large moving objects, *EURASIP Journal on Image and Video Processing*, 2:2019. DOI: 10.1186/s13640-018-0380-9. 18

[111] E. Chen, O. Haik, and Y. Yitzhaky, Online spatio-temporal action detection in long-distance imaging affected by the atmosphere, *IEEE Access*, 9:24531–24545, 2021. DOI: 10.1109/access.2021.3057172. 18

[112] D. Droege, R. Hardie, B. Allen, A. Dapore, and J. Blevins, A real-time atmospheric turbulence mitigation and super-resolution solution for infrared imaging systems, *Proc. SPIE*, 8355, 2012. DOI: 10.1117/12.920323. 18

[113] R. Hardie, M. Rucci, B. Karch, A. Dapore, D. Droege, and J. French, Fusion of interpolated frames superresolution in the presence of atmospheric optical turbulence, *SPIE Optical Engineering*, 58(8):157–170, 2019. DOI: 10.1117/1.oe.58.8.083103. 18

[114] K. Gibson and T. Nguyen, An analysis and method for contrast enhancement turbulence mitigation, *IEEE Transactions on Image Processing*, 23(7):3179–3190, 2014. DOI: 10.1109/tip.2014.2328180. 18

[115] M.-T. Velluet, C. Bell, J.-F. Daigle, J. Dijk, S. Gladysz, A. Kanaev, A. Lambert, D. LeMaster, G. Potvin, and M. Vorontsov, Data collection and preliminary results on turbulence characterisation and mitigation techniques, *Proc. SPIE*, 11159, 2019. DOI: 10.1117/12.2533821. 18

[116] A. van Eekeren, K. Schutte, J. Dijk, and P. Schwering, Quantitative evaluation of turbulence compensation, *Proc. SPIE*, 8706, 2013. DOI: 10.1117/12.2015371. 18

[117] A. van Eekeren, K. Schutte, and L. van Vliet, Multiframe super-resolution reconstruction of small moving objects, *IEEE Transactions on Image Processing*, 19(11):2901–2912, 2010. DOI: 10.1109/tip.2010.2068210. 19, 20

[118] L. Yue, H. Shen, J. Li, Q. Yuan, H. Zhang, and L. Zhang, Image super-resolution: The techniques, applications, and future, *Signal Processing*, 128:389–408, 2016. DOI: 10.1016/j.sigpro.2016.05.002. 19

[119] T. Y. Han, Y. J. Kim, and B. C. Song, Convolutional neural network-based infrared image super resolution under low light environment, *European Signal Processing Conference (EUSIPCO)*, 2017. DOI: 10.23919/eusipco.2017.8081318. 19

[120] Z. Wang, J. Chen, and S. C. H. Hoi, Deep learning for image super-resolution: A survey, *IEEE Transactions on Pattern Analysis and Machine Intelligence (TPAMI)*, Early Access, 2020. DOI: 10.1016/j.neucom.2019.09.091. 19

[121] S. Farsiu, M. Robinson, M. Elad, and P. Milanfar, Fast and robust multiframe super resolution, *IEEE Transactions on Image Processing (TIP)*, 13:1327–1344, 2004. DOI: 10.1109/tip.2004.834669. 19

[122]  M. Irani and S. Peleg, Improving resolution by image registration, *Graphical Models and Image Processing*, 53:231–239, 1991. DOI: 10.1016/1049-9652(91)90045-l. 19

[123]  R. Tsai, Multiframe image restoration and registration, *Advance Computer Visual and Image Processing*, 1:317–333, 1984. 19

[124]  A. Molini, D. Valsesia, G. Fracastoro, and E. Magli, DeepSUM: Deep neural network for super-resolution of unregistered multitemporal images, *IEEE Transactions on Geoscience and Remote Sensing (TGRS)*, 58:3644–3365, 2019. DOI: 10.1109/tgrs.2019.2959248. 19

[125]  M. Deudon, A. Kalaitzis, I. Goytom, M. Arefin, Z. Lin, K. Sankaran, V. Michalski, S. Kahou, J. Cornebise, and Y. Bengio, Highres-net: Recursive fusion for multi-frame super-resolution of satellite imagery, *ArXiv Preprint ArXiv:2002.06460*, 2020. 19

[126]  H. Chang, D. Yeung, and Y. Xiong, Super-resolution through neighbor embedding, *IEEE CVPR*, 2004. DOI: 10.1109/cvpr.2004.1315043. 19

[127]  D. Glasner, S. Bagon, and M. Irani, Super-resolution from a single image, *IEEE International Conference on Computer Vision*, pages 349–356, 2009. DOI: 10.1109/iccv.2009.5459271. 19

[128]  X. Yu, B. Fernando, R. Hartley, and F. Porikli, Super-resolving very low-resolution face images with supplementary attributes, *IEEE CVPR*, 2018. DOI: 10.1109/cvpr.2018.00101. 19

[129]  J. Dijk, K. Schutte, A. van Eekeren, and P. Bijl, Measuring the performance of super-resolution reconstruction algorithms, *Proc. of SPIE*, 8355, 2012. DOI: 10.1117/12.919225. 19

[130]  A. Mehri, P. B. Ardakani, and A. D. Sappa, MPRNet: Multi-path residual network for lightweight image super resolution, *IEEE Winter Conference on Applied Computer Vision (WACV)*, 2021. DOI: 10.1109/wacv48630.2021.00275. 20

[131]  E. Mandanici, L. Tavasci, F. Corsini, and S. Gandolfi, A multi-image super-resolution algorithm applied to thermal imagery, *Applied Geomatics*, 11:215–228, 2019. DOI: 10.1007/s12518-019-00253-y. 20

[132]  F. Salvetti, V. Mazzia, A. Khaliq, and M. Chiaberge, Multi-image super resolution of remotely sensed images using residual attention deep neural networks, *Remote Sensing*, 12:1–20, 2020. DOI: 10.3390/rs12142207. 20

[133]  Y. Choi, N. Kim, S. Hwang, and I. Kweon, Thermal image enhancement using convolutional neural network, *Intelligent Robots and Systems (IROS)*, 2016. DOI: 10.1109/iros.2016.7759059. 20

[134] C. Dong, C. Loy, K. He, and X. Tang, Image super-resolution using deep convolutional networks, *IEEE Transactions on Pattern Analysis and Machine Intelligence (TPAMI)*, 38(2):295–307, 2016. DOI: 10.1109/tpami.2015.2439281. 20

[135] R. Rivadeneira, A. Sappa, B. Vintimilla, L. Guo, J. Hou, A. Mehri, P. Ardakani, H. Patel, V. Chudasama, K. Prajapati, K. Upla, R. Ramachandra, K. Raja, C. Busch, F. Almasri, O. Debeir, S. Nathan, P. Kansal, N. Gutierrez, B. Mojra, and W. Beksi, Thermal image super-resolution challenge—PBVS, *IEEE CVPR Workshops*, 2020. DOI: 10.1109/cvprw50498.2020.00056. 21

[136] J. Poujol, C. A. Aguilera, E. Danos, B. Vintimilla, R. Toledo, and A. D. Sappa, A visible-thermal fusion based monocular visual odometry. *Second Iberian Robotics Conference*, 2015. DOI: 10.1007/978-3-319-27146-0_40. 26, 74

[137] X. Chen, P. J. Flynn, and K. W. Bowyer, Visible-light and infrared face recognition, *ACM Workshop on Multimodal User Authentication*, 2003. 25, 67

[138] J. Davis and V. Sharma, Background-subtraction using contour-based fusion of thermal and visible imagery, *Computer Vision and Image Understanding*, 106:162–182, 2007. DOI: 10.1016/j.cviu.2006.06.010. 25, 42, 43, 45

[139] M. Brown and S. Süsstrunk, Multi-spectral SIFT for scene category recognition, *IEEE CVPR*, 2011. DOI: 10.1109/cvpr.2011.5995637. 25, 29

[140] F. Barrera, F. Lumbreras, and A. Sappa, Multimodal stereo vision system: 3D data extraction and algorithm evaluation, *IEEE Journal of Selected Topics in Signal Processing*, 6:437–446, 2012. DOI: 10.1109/jstsp.2012.2204036. 25

[141] F. Barrera, F. Lumbreras, and A. Sappa, Multispectral piecewise planar stereo using Manhattan-world assumption, *Pattern Recognition Letters*, 34:52–61, 2013. DOI: 10.1016/j.patrec.2012.08.009. 25

[142] F. Bilodeau, A. Torabi, P. St-Charles, and D. Riahi, Thermal-visible registration of human silhouettes: A similarity measure performance evaluation, *Infrared Physics and Technology*, 64:79–86, 2014. DOI: 10.1016/j.infrared.2014.02.005. 25

[143] M. M. Zhang, J. Choi, K. Daniilidis, M. T. Wolf, and C. Kanan, VAIS: A dataset for recognizing maritime imagery in the visible and infrared spectrums, *IEEE CVPR Workshops*, 2015. DOI: 10.1109/cvprw.2015.7301291. 25, 43

[144] J. Lüthen, J. Wörmann, M. Kleinsteuber, and J. Steurer, A RGB/NIR data set for evaluating dehazing algorithms, *Electronic Imaging*, 2017:79–87, 2017. DOI: 10.2352/issn.2470-1173.2017.12.iqsp-229. 25, 32, 33

[145] Y. Choi, N. Kim, S. Hwang, K. Park, J. Yoon K. An, and I. Kweon, KAIST multi-spectral day/night data set for autonomous and assisted driving, *IEEE Transactions on Intelligent Transportation Systems*, 19:934–948, 2018. DOI: 10.1109/tits.2018.2791533. 25, 29, 79

[146] C. Li, X. Liang, Y. Lu, N. Zhao, and J. Tang, RGB-T object tracking: Benchmark and baseline, *Pattern Recognition*, 96:2019. DOI: 10.1016/j.patcog.2019.106977. 25, 51, 52

[147] S. Zhang, X. Wang, A. Liu, C. Zhao, J. Wan, S. Escalera, H. Shi, Z. Wang, and S. Li, A dataset and benchmark for large-scale multimodal face anti-spoofing, *IEEE CVPR Workshops*, 2019. DOI: 10.1109/cvpr.2019.00101. 25

[148] Q. Wan, S. Agaian, S. Rajeev, S. Kamath, R. Rajendran, S. Rao, A. Kaszowska, H. Taylor, A. Samani, and X. Yuan, A comprehensive database for benchmarking imaging systems, *IEEE Transactions on Pattern Analysis and Machine Intelligence*, 42(3):509–520, 2020. DOI: 10.1109/tpami.2018.2884458. 25, 67, 68, 69

[149] H. Le, C. Smailis, L. Shi, and I. Kakadiaris, EDGE20: A cross spectral evaluation dataset for multiple surveillance problems, *IEEE Winter Conference on Applications of Computer Vision (WACV)*, 2020. DOI: 10.1109/wacv45572.2020.9093573. 25

[150] J. Vertens, J. Zürn, and W. Burgard, HeatNet: Bridging the day-night domain gap in semantic segmentation with thermal images, *ArXiv:2003.04645*, 2020. DOI: 10.1109/iros45743.2020.9341192. 25, 57

[151] B. Zitova and J. Flusser, Image registration methods: A survey, *Image and Vision Computing*, 21:977–1000, 2003. DOI: 10.1016/s0262-8856(03)00137-9. 23, 25, 38

[152] D. Firmenichy, M. Brown, and S. Süsstrunk, Multispectral interest points for RGB-NIR image registration, *IEEE International Conference on Image Processing (ICIP)*, 2011. DOI: 10.1109/icip.2011.6115818. 25

[153] C. Aguilera, F. Barrera, F. Lumbreras, A. Sappa, and R. Toledo, Multispectral image feature points, *Sensors*, 12:12661–72, 2012. DOI: 10.3390/s120912661. 25, 26

[154] D. G. Lowe, Distinctive image features from scale-invariant keypoints, *International Journal of Computer Vision (IJCV)*, 60(2):91–110, 2004. DOI: 10.1023/b:visi.0000029664.99615.94. 26, 37

[155] B. S.. Manjunath, J. R. Ohm, V. V. Vasudevan, and A. Yamada, Color and texture descriptors, *IEEE Transactions on Circuits and Systems for Video Technology*, 11(6):703–715, 2001. DOI: 10.1109/76.927424. 26

[156] S. Sonn, G.-A. Bilodeau, and P. Galinier, Fast and accurate registration of visible and infrared videos, *IEEE CVPR Workshops*, 2013. DOI: 10.1109/cvprw.2013.53. 26

[157] S. J. Krotosky and M. M. Trivedi, Mutual information-based registration of multi-modal stereo videos for person tracking, *Computer Vision and Image Understanding (CVIU)*, 106:270–287, 2007. DOI: 10.1016/j.cviu.2006.10.008. 26, 74

[158] D.-L. Nguyen, P.-L. St-Charles, and G.-A. Bilodeau, Non-planar infrared-visible registration for uncalibrated stereo pairs, *IEEE CVPR Workshops*, 2016. DOI: 10.1109/cvprw.2016.48. 26

[159] C. Aguilera, A. Sappa, and R. Toledo, LGHD: A feature descriptor for matching across non-linear intensity variations, *IEEE International Conference on Image Processing (ICIP)*, 2015. DOI: 10.1109/icip.2015.7350783. 26

[160] C. Aguilera, A. Sappa, C. Agulera, and R. Toledo, Cross-spectral local descriptors via quadruplet network, *Sensors*, 17:1–14, 2017. DOI: 10.3390/s17040873. 27

[161] V. Balntas, E. Johns, L. Tang, and K. Mikolajczyk, PN-Net: Conjoined triple deep network for learning local image descriptors, *ArXiv:1601.05030.*, 2016. 27

[162] D. Quan, X. Liang, S. Wang, S. Wei, Y. Li, N. Huyan, and L. Jiao, AFD-Net: Aggregated feature difference learning for cross-spectral image patch matching, *IEEE International Conference on Computer Vision (ICCV)*, 2019. DOI: 10.1109/iccv.2019.00311. 27

[163] S. Kim, D. Min, S. Lin, and K. Sohn, Dense cross-modal correspondence estimation with the deep self-correlation descriptor, *IEEE Transactions on Pattern Analysis and Machine Intelligence*, Early Access, 2020. DOI: 10.1109/tpami.2020.2965528. 27

[164] V. G. Jacob and S. Gupta, Colorization of grayscale images and videos using a semiautomatic approach, *IEEE International Conference on Image Processing (ICIP)*, 2009. DOI: 10.1109/icip.2009.5413392. 28

[165] A. Bugeau and V.-T. Ta, Patch-based image colorization, *International Conference on Pattern Recognition (ICPR)*, 2012. 28

[166] S. Xia, J. Liu, Y. Fang, W. Yang, and Z. Guo, Robust and automatic video colorization via multiframe reordering refinement, *IEEE International Conference on Image Processing (ICIP)*, 2016. DOI: 10.1109/icip.2016.7533114. 28

[167] A. Deshpande, J. Rock, and D. Forsyth, Learning large-scale automatic image colorization, *IEEE International Conference on Computer Vision (ICCV)*, 2015. DOI: 10.1109/iccv.2015.72. 28

[168] D. Varga and T. Sziranyi, Fully automatic image colorization based on convolutional neural network, *International Conference on Pattern Recognition (ICPR)*, 2016. DOI: 10.1109/icpr.2016.7900208. 28

[169] M. Kieu, L. Berlincioni, L. Galteri, M. Bertini, A. Bagdanov, and A. Del Bimbo, Robust pedestrian detection in thermal imagery using synthesized images, *International Conference on Pattern Recognition (ICPR)*, 2021. DOI: 10.1109/icpr48806.2021.9412764. 28, 48

[170] L. Zhang, A. Gonzalez-Garcia, J. van de Weijer, M. Danelljan, and F. S. Khan, Synthetic data generation for end-to-end thermal infrared tracking, *IEEE Transactions on Image Processing*, 28(4):1837–1850, 2018. DOI: 10.1109/tip.2018.2879249. 28

[171] M. Limmer and H. Lensch, Infrared colorization using deep convolutional neural networks, *IEEE International Conference on Machine Learning and Applications (ICMLA)*, 2016. DOI: 10.1109/icmla.2016.0019. 29

[172] A. Berg, J. Ahlberg, and M. Felsberg, Generating visible spectrum images from thermal infrared, *IEEE CVPR Workshops*, 2018. DOI: 10.1109/cvprw.2018.00159. 29

[173] Z. Dong, S. Kamata, and T. Breckon, Infrared image colorization using a s-shape network, *IEEE International Conference on Image Processing (ICIP)*, 2018. DOI: 10.1109/icip.2018.8451230. 29

[174] I. Goodfellow, J. Pouget-Abadie, M. Mirza, B. Xu, D. Warde-Farley S. Ozair, A. Courville, and Y. Bengio, Generative adversarial nets, *Advances in Neural Information Processing Systems (NIPS)*, 2014. 29

[175] P. Isola, J. Zhu, T. Zhou, and A. Efros, Image-to-image translation with conditional adversarial networks, *IEEE Conference on Computer Vision and Pattern Recognition (CVPR)*, 2017. DOI: 10.1109/cvpr.2017.632. 29

[176] P. L. Suárez, A. D. Sappa, and B. X. Vintimilla, Infrared image colorization based on a triplet DCGAN architecture, *IEEE CVPR Workshops*, 2017. DOI: 10.1109/cvprw.2017.32. 29

[177] X. Kuang, J. Zhu, X. Sui, Y. Liu, C. Liu, Q. Chen, and G. Gu, Thermal infrared colorization via conditional generative adversarial network, *Infrared Physics and Technology*, 107:1–8, 2020. DOI: 10.1016/j.infrared.2020.103338. 29

[178] J. Zhu, T. Park, P. Isola, and A. Efros, Unpaired image-to-image translation using cycle-consistent adversarial networks, *IEEE International Conference on Computer Vision (ICCV)*, 2017. DOI: 10.1109/iccv.2017.244. 29

[179] A. Mehri and A. Sappa, Colorizing near infrared images through a cyclic adversarial approach of unpaired samples, *IEEE CVPR Workshops*, 2019. DOI: 10.1109/cvprw.2019.00128. 29, 30

[180] A. Gijsenij, T. Gevers, and M. Lucassen, A perceptual comparison of distance measures for color constancy algorithms, *European Conference on Computer Vision (ECCV)*, 2008. DOI: 10.1007/978-3-540-88682-2_17. 31

[181] X. Chen, G. Zhai, J. Wang, C. Hu, and Y. Chen, Color guided thermal image super resolution, *IEEE Visual Communications and Image Processing (VCIP)*, 2016. DOI: 10.1109/vcip.2016.7805509. 31

[182] Y. Choi, N. Kim, S. Hwang, and I. Kweon, Thermal image enhancement using convolutional neural network, *IEEE International Conference on Intelligent Robots and Systems (IROS)*, 2016. DOI: 10.1109/iros.2016.7759059. 31

[183] H. Gupta and K. Mitra, Pyramidal edge-maps and attention-based guided thermal super-resolution, *European Conference on Computer Vision (ECCV)*, 2020. DOI: 10.1007/978-3-030-67070-2_42. 31, 32

[184] F. Almasari and O. Debeir, Multimodal sensor fusion in single thermal image super-resolution, *Asian Conference on Computer Vision (ACCV)*, 2018. DOI: 10.1007/978-3-030-21074-8_34. 31

[185] Z. Jingyun, D. Yifan, Y. Yi, and S. Jiasong, Real-time defog model based on visible and near-infrared information, *IEEE International Conference on Multimedia and Expo Workshops (ICMEW)*, 2016. DOI: 10.1109/icmew.2016.7574749. 32

[186] Y. Kudo and A. Kubota, Image dehazing method by fusing weighted near-infrared image, *International Workshop on Advanced Image Technology (IWAIT)*, 2018 DOI: 10.1109/iwait.2018.8369744. 32

[187] A. Vanmali, S. Kelkar, and V. Gadre, A novel approach for image dehazing combining visible-NIR images, *IEEE 5th National Conference on Computer Vision, Pattern Recognition, Image Processing and Graphics (NCVPRIPG)*, 2015. DOI: 10.1109/ncvpripg.2015.7489945. 32

[188] C. Son and X. Zhang, Near-infrared fusion via color regularization for haze and color distortion removals, *IEEE Transactions on Circuits and Systems for Video Technology*, 28:3111–3126, 2017. DOI: 10.1109/tcsvt.2017.2748150. 33

[189] T. Shibata, M. Tanaka, and M. Okutomi, Misalignment-robust joint filter for cross-modal image pairs, *IEEE International Conference on Computer Vision (ICCV)*, 2017. DOI: 10.1109/iccv.2017.357. 33

[190] S. Zhuo, X. Zhang, X. Miao, and T. Sim, Enhancing low light images using near infrared flash images, *IEEE International Conference on Image Processing (ICIP)*, 2010. DOI: 10.1109/icip.2010.5652900. 33

[191] H. Honda, R. Timofte, and L. van Gool, Make my day—high-fidelity color denoising with near-infrared, *IEEE CVPR Workshops*, 2015. DOI: 10.1109/cvprw.2015.7301300. 33

[192] K. Dabov, A. Foi, V. Katkovnik, and K. Egiazarian, Image denoising by sparse 3D transform-domain collaborative filtering, *IEEE Transactions on Image Processing*, 16(8):2080–2095, 2007. DOI: 10.1109/tip.2007.901238. 34

[193] X. Soria and A. Sappa, Improving edge detection in RGB images by adding NIR chan-nel, *International Conference on Signal-Image Technology and Internet-Based Systems (SITIS)*, 2018. DOI: 10.1109/sitis.2018.00048. 34

[194] S. Xie and Z. Tu, Holistically-nested edge detection, *International Journal of Computer Vision (IJCV)*, 125:3–18, 2017. DOI: 10.1007/s11263-017-1004-z. 34

[195] M. El Helou, Z. Sadeghipoor, and S. Süsstrunk, Correlation-based deblurring leveraging multispectral chromatic aberration in color and near-infrared joint acquisition, *IEEE ICIP*, 2017. DOI: 10.1109/icip.2017.8296512. 34

[196] K. He, X. Zhang, S. Ren, and J. Sun, Deep residual learning for image recognition, *IEEE CVPR*, 2016. DOI: 10.1109/cvpr.2016.90. 35

[197] J. Cao, H. Cholakkal, R. M. Anwer, F. S. Khan, Y. Pang, and L. Shao, D2Det: To-wards high quality object detection and instance segmentation, *IEEE CVPR*, 2020. DOI: 10.1109/cvpr42600.2020.01150. 35

[198] Y. Yang, A. Loquercio, D. Scaramuzza, and S. Soatto, Unsupervised moving object detection via contextual information separation, *IEEE CVPR*, 2019. DOI: 10.1109/cvpr.2019.00097. 35

[199] H. Meuel, Analysis of affine motion-compensated prediction and its application in aerial video coding, Dissertation, Leibniz University Hannover, Hannover, Germany, 2019. DOI: 10.51202/9783186865106. 35

[200] D. Kaufman, G. Levi, T. Hassner, and L. Wolf, Temporal tessellation: A unified approach for video analysis, *IEEE ICCV*, 2017. DOI: 10.1109/iccv.2017.20. 35

[201] A. Miech, D. Zhukov, J.-B. Alayrac, M. Tapaswi, I. Laptev, and J. Sivic, HowTo100M: Learning a text-video embedding by watching hundred million narrated video clips, *IEEE ICCV*, 2019. DOI: 10.1109/iccv.2019.00272. 35

[202] A. Bovik et al., *Handbook of Image and Video Processing*, Elsevier Academic Press, 2005. 35

[203] L. Liu, W. Ouyang, X. Wang, P. Fieguth, J. Chen, X. Liu, and M. Pietikäinen, Deep learning for generic object detection: A survey, *International Journal of Computer Vision*, 128:261–318, 2020. DOI: 10.1007/s11263-019-01247-4. 35

[204] S. Minaee, Y. Boykov, F. Porikli, A. Plaza, N. Kehtarnavaz, and D. Terzopoulos, Image segmentation using deep learning: A survey, *ArXiv:2001.05566*, 2020. DOI: 10.1109/tpami.2021.3059968. 35

[205] H. Bae et al., IROS 2019 lifelong robotic vision: Object recognition challenge, *IEEE Robotics and Automation Magazine*, 27(2):11–16, 2020. DOI: 10.1109/mra.2020.2987186. 35

[206] S. Sivaraman and M. M. Trivedi, Looking at vehicles on the road: A survey of vision-based vehicle detection, tracking, and behavior analysis, *IEEE Transactions Intelligent Transportation Systems*, 14(4):1773–1795, 2013. DOI: 10.1109/tits.2013.2266661. 35, 49

[207] E. Yurtsever, J. Lambert, A. Carballo, and K. Takeda, A survey of autonomous driving: Common practices and emerging technologies, *IEEE Access*, 8:58443–58469, 2020. DOI: 10.1109/access.2020.2983149. 35

[208] Q. Zhang, H. Sun, X. Wu, and H. Zhong, Edge video analytics for public safety: A review, *Proc. of the IEEE*, 107(8):1675–1696, 2019. DOI: 10.1109/jproc.2019.2925910. 35, 75

[209] N. Goyette, P.-M. Jodoin, F. Porikli, J. Konrad, and P. Ishwar, Changedetection.net: A new change detection benchmark dataset, *IEEE CVPR Workshops*, 2012. DOI: 10.1109/cvprw.2012.6238919. 36

[210] Y. Wang, P.-M. Jodoin, F. Porikli, J. Konrad, Y. Benezeth, and P. Ishwar, CDnet 2014: An expanded change detection benchmark dataset, *IEEE CVPR Workshops*, 2014. DOI: 10.1109/cvprw.2014.126. 36, 37, 63

[211] M. Dillencourt, H. Samet, and M. Tamminen, A general approach to connected-component labeling for arbitrary image representations, *Journal of the ACM*, 39(2):253–280, 1992. DOI: 10.1145/128749.128750. 37

[212] D. Martin, C. Fowlkes, D. Tal, and J. Malik, A database of human segmented natural images and its application to evaluating segmentation algorithms and measuring ecological statistics, *IEEE International Conference on Computer Vision (ICCV)*, 2001. DOI: 10.1109/iccv.2001.937655. 37

[213] P. Arbelaez, M. Maire, C. Fowlkes, and J. Malik, Contour detection and hierarchical image segmentation, *IEEE Transactions on Pattern Analysis and Machine Intelligence*, 33(5):898–916, 2011. DOI: 10.1109/tpami.2010.161. 37

[214] J. Shi and C. Tomasi, Good features to track, *IEEE CVPR*, 1994. DOI: 10.1109/cvpr.1994.323794. 37

[215] H. Bay, T. Tuytelaars, and L. van Gool, SURF: Speeded up robust features, *European Conference on Computer Vision (ECCV)*, 2006. DOI: 10.1007/11744023_32. 37

[216] R. Hartley and A. Zisserman, *Multiple-View Geometry in Computer Vision*, Cambridge University Press, 2004. DOI: 10.1023/A:1008162616689. 37

[217] M. Brown and D. G. Lowe, Automatic panoramic image stitching using invariant features, *International Journal of Computer Vision (IJCV)*, 74(1):59–73, 2007. DOI: 10.1007/s11263-006-0002-3. 37

[218] F. Zhang and F. Liu, Parallax-tolerant image stitching, *IEEE CVPR*, 2014. DOI: 10.1109/cvpr.2014.423. 37

[219] C. Stauffer and W. Grimson, Adaptive background mixture models for real-time tracking, *IEEE CVPR*, 1999. DOI: 10.1109/cvpr.1999.784637. 38

[220] Z. Zivkovic, Improved adaptive Gaussian mixture model for background subtraction, *International Conference on Pattern Recognition (ICPR)*, 2004. DOI: 10.1109/icpr.2004.1333992. 38

[221] O. Barnich and M. Van Droogenbroeck, ViBe: A universal background subtraction algorithm for video sequences, *IEEE Transactions on Image Processing*, 20(6):1709–1724, 2011. DOI: 10.1109/tip.2010.2101613. 38

[222] V. Reilly, H. Idrees, and M. Shah, Detection and tracking of large number of targets in wide area surveillance, *European Conference on Computer Vision (ECCV)*, 2010. DOI: 10.1007/978-3-642-15558-1_14. 38, 62

[223] L. W. Sommer, M. Teutsch, T. Schuchert, and J. Beyerer, A survey on moving object detection for wide area motion imagery, *IEEE Winter Conference on Applications of Computer Vision (WACV)*, 2016. DOI: 10.1109/wacv.2016.7477573. 38, 62

[224] T. Bouwmans, Traditional and recent approaches in background modeling for foreground detection: An overview, *Computer Science Review*, 11–12:31–66, 2014. DOI: 10.1016/j.cosrev.2014.04.001. 38

[225] T. Bouwmans, F. Porikli, B. Höferlin, and A. Vacavant (Eds.), *Background Modeling and Foreground Detection for Video Surveillance*, CRC Press, 2014. DOI: 10.1201/b17223. 38

[226] G. Saur, W. Krüger, and A. Schumann, Extended image differencing for change detection in UAV video mosaics, *Proc. of SPIE*, 9026, 2014. DOI: 10.1117/12.2043209. 38

[227] M. Narayana, A. Hanson, and E. Learned-Miller, Coherent motion segmentation in moving camera videos using optical flow orientations, *IEEE ICCV*, 2013. DOI: 10.1109/iccv.2013.199. 38

[228] Y. Chen, J. Wang, B. Zhu, M. Tang, and H. Lu, Pixel-wise deep sequence learning for moving object detection, *IEEE Transactions on Circuits and Systems for Video Technology*, Early Access, 2017. DOI: 10.1109/tcsvt.2017.2770319. 39

[229] T. Bouwmans, S. Javed, M. Sultana, and S. K. Jung, Deep neural network concepts for background subtraction: A systematic review and comparative evaluation, *Neural Networks*, 117:8–66, 2018. DOI: 10.1016/j.neunet.2019.04.024. 39

[230] T. P. Nguyen, C. C. Pham, S. V.-U. Ha, and J. W. Jeon, Change detection by training a triplet network for motion feature extraction, *IEEE Transactions on Circuits and Systems for Video Technology*, Early Access, 2018. DOI: 10.1109/tcsvt.2018.2795657. 39

[231] M. Babaee, D. Dinh, and G. Rigoll, A deep convolutional neural network for video sequence background subtraction, *Pattern Recognition*, 76:635–649, 2018. DOI: 10.1016/j.patcog.2017.09.040. 39

[232] L. A Lim and H. Y. Keles, Foreground segmentation using convolutional neural networks for multiscale feature encoding, *Pattern Recognition Letters*, 112:256–262, 2018. DOI: 10.1016/j.patrec.2018.08.002. 39

[233] M. O. Tezcan, P. Ishwar, and J. Konrad, BSUV-Net: A fully-convolutional neural network for background subtraction of unseen videos, *IEEE Winter Conference on Applied Computer Vision (WACV)*, 2020. DOI: 10.1109/wacv45572.2020.9093464. 39

[234] M. Mandal and S. K. Vipparthi, Scene independency matters: An empirical study of scene dependent and scene independent evaluation for CNN-based change detection, *IEEE Transactions on Intelligent Transportation Systems*, Early Access, 2020. DOI: 10.1109/tits.2020.3030801. 39

[235] T. Akilan, Q. Wu, A. Safaei, J. Huo, and Y. Yang, A 3D CNN-LSTM-based image-to-image foreground segmentation, *IEEE Transactions on Intelligent Transportation Systems*, 21(3):959–971, 2020. DOI: 10.1109/tits.2019.2900426. 39

[236] M. Braham, S. Pierard, and M. Van Droogenbroeck, Semantic background subtraction, *IEEE International Conference on Image Processing (ICIP)*, 2017. DOI: 10.1109/icip.2017.8297144. 39

[237] J. Vertens, A. Valada, and W. Burgard, SMSnet: Semantic motion segmentation using deep convolutional neural networks, *IEEE International Conference on Intelligent Robots and Systems (IROS)*, 2017. DOI: 10.1109/iros.2017.8202211. 39

[238] A. Ess, K. Schindler, B. Leibe, and L. van Gool, Object detection and tracking for autonomous navigation in dynamic environments, *International Journal of Robotics Research (IJRR)*, 29(14):1707–1725, 2010. DOI: 10.1177/0278364910365417. 39

[239] F. Yang, A. Kale, Y. Bubnov, L. Stein, Q. Wang, H. Kiapour, and R. Piramuthu, Visual search at ebay, *ACM International Conference on Knowledge Discovery and Data Mining (SIGKDD)*, 2017. DOI: 10.1145/3097983.3098162. 39

[240] X. Geng, H. Zhang, J. Bian, and T. Chua, Learning image and user features for recommendation in social networks, *IEEE International Conference on Computer Vision (ICCV)*, 2015. DOI: 10.1109/iccv.2015.486. 39

[241] T. Chen, L. Ravindranath, S. Deng, P. Bahl, and H. Balakrishnan, Glimpse: Continuous, real-time object recognition on mobile devices, *ACM Conference on Embedded Networked Sensor Systems*, 2015. DOI: 10.1145/2809695.2809711. 39

[242] D. Parikh, C. L. Zitnick, and T. Chen, Exploring tiny images: The roles of appearance and contextual information for machine and human object recognition, *IEEE Transactions on Pattern Analysis and Machine Intelligence*, 34(10):1978–1991, 2012. DOI: 10.1109/tpami.2011.276. 40

[243] J. Ge, Y. Luo, and G. Tei, Real-time pedestrian detection and tracking at nighttime for driver-assistance systems, *IEEE Transactions on Intelligent Transportation Systems*, 10(2):283–298, 2009. DOI: 10.1109/tits.2009.2018961. 40, 45, 73

[244] A. Gaszczak, T. P. Breckon, and J. Han, Real-time people and vehicle detection from UAV imagery, *Proc. of SPIE*, 7878, 2011. DOI: 10.1117/12.876663. 40, 46

[245] M. San-Biagio, M. Crocco, M. Cristani, S. Martelli, and V. Murino, Low-level multimodal integration on Riemannian manifolds for automatic pedestrian detection, *International Conference on Information Fusion*, 2012. 40

[246] O. Russakovsky, J. Deng, H. Su, J. Krause, S. Satheesh, S. Ma, Z. Huang, A. Karpathy, A. Khosla, M. Bernstein, A. C. Berg, and L. Fei-Fei, ImageNet large scale visual recognition challenge, *International Journal of Computer Vision (IJCV)*, 115(3):211–252, 2015. DOI: 10.1007/s11263-015-0816-y. 40

[247] M. Everingham, S. M. A. Eslami, L. Van Gool, C. K. I. Williams, J. Winn, and A. Zisserman, ImageNet large scale visual recognition challenge, *International Journal of Computer Vision (IJCV)*, 111(1):98–136, 2015. DOI: 10.1007/s11263-015-0816-y. 40, 42

[248] T. Fawcett, An introduction to ROC analysis, *Pattern Recognition Letters*, 27:861–874, 2006. DOI: 10.1016/j.patrec.2005.10.010. 41

[249] R. Kasturi, D. Goldof, P. Soundararajan, V. Manohar, J. Garofolo, R. Bowers, M. Boonstra, V. Korzhova, and J. Zhang, Framework for performance evaluation of face, text, and vehicle detection and tracking in video: Data, metrics, and protocol, *IEEE Transactions on Pattern Analysis and Machine Intelligence*, 31(2):319–336, 2009. DOI: 10.1109/tpami.2008.57. 41, 42, 50

[250] R. Padilla, W. Passos, T. Dias, S. Netto, and E. da Silva, A comparative analysis of object detection metrics with a companion open-source toolkit, *Electronics*, 10(3), 2021. DOI: 10.3390/electronics10030279. 41

[251] T. Y. Lin, M. Maire, S. Belongie, J. Hays, P. Perona, D. Ramanan, P. Dollár, and C. L. Zitnick, Microsoft COCO: Common objects in context, *European Conference on Computer Vision (ECCV)*, 2014. DOI: 10.1007/978-3-319-10602-1_48. 41

[252] P. Dollár, C. Wojek, B. Schiele, P. Perona, Pedestrian detection: An evaluation of the state-of-the-art, *IEEE Transactions on Pattern Analysis and Machine Intelligence*, 34(4):743–761, 2012. DOI: 10.1109/tpami.2011.155. 41, 42

[253] J. Davis and M. Keck, A two-stage template approach to person detection in thermal imagery, *IEEE WACV/MOTION*, 2005. DOI: 10.1109/ACVMOT.2005.14. 42, 43, 45, 46, 65

[254] R. Miezianko, Terravic research infrared database, *IEEE OTCBVS WS Series Bench*, 2006. 42, 43, 65, 67

[255] A. Akula, R. Ghosh, S. Kumar, and H. K. Sardana, Moving target detection in thermal infrared imagery using spatiotemporal information, *Journal of the Optical Society of America (JOSA)*, 30(8):1492–1501, 2013. DOI: 10.1364/josaa.30.001492. 42, 43

[256] J. Portmann, S. Lynen, M. Chli, and R. Siegwart, People detection and tracking from aerial thermal views, *IEEE International Conference on Robotics and Automation (ICRA)*, 2014. DOI: 10.1109/icra.2014.6907094. 42, 43, 51, 52, 56

[257] D. Bloisi, L. Iocchi, A. Pennisi, and L. Tombolini, ARGOS-Venice boat classification, *IEEE International Conference on Advance Video and Signal-Based Surveillance (AVSS)*, 2015. DOI: 10.1109/avss.2015.7301727. 43, 51

[258] D. K. Prasad, D. Rajan, L. Rachmawati, E. Rajabaly, and C. Quek, Video processing from electro-optical sensors for object detection and tracking in maritime environment: A survey, *IEEE Transactions on Intelligent Transportation Systems*, 18(8):1993–2016, 2017. DOI: 10.1109/tits.2016.2634580. 43, 51

[259] S. K. Biswas and P. Milanfar, Linear support tensor machine with LSK channels: Pedestrian detection in thermal infrared images, *IEEE Transactions on Image Processing*, 26(9):4229–4242, 2017. DOI: 10.1109/tip.2017.2705426. 42, 46

[260] A. Leykin, Y. Ran, and R. Hammoud, Thermal-visible video fusion for moving target tracking and pedestrian classification, *IEEE CVPR*, 2007. DOI: 10.1109/cvpr.2007.383444. 39, 43, 45, 56

[261] C. Papageorgiou and T. Poggio, A trainable system for object detection, *International Journal of Computer Vision, IEEE International Conference on Computer Vision (ICCV)*, 2000. 44

[262] P. Viola and M. Jones, Rapid object detection using a boosted cascade of simple features, *IEEE CVPR*, 2001. DOI: 10.1109/cvpr.2001.990517. 44, 45

[263] N. Dalal and B. Triggs, Histograms of oriented gradients for human detection, *IEEE CVPR*, 2005. DOI: 10.1109/cvpr.2005.177. 44, 45

[264] P. Dollár, Z. Tu, P. Perona, and S. Belongie Integral channel features, *British Machine Vision Conference (BMVC)*, 2009. DOI: 10.5244/c.23.91. 44, 46

[265] R. Benenson, M. Mathias, T. Tuytelaars, and L. Van Gool, Seeking the strongest rigid detector, *IEEE CVPR*, 2013. DOI: 10.1109/cvpr.2013.470. 45

[266] P. Dollár, R. Appel, S. Belongie, and P. Perona, Fast feature pyramids for object detection, *IEEE Transactions on Pattern Analysis and Machine Intelligence*, 36(8):1532–1545, 2014. DOI: 10.1109/tpami.2014.2300479. 45, 46

[267] R. Benenson, M. Mathias, R. Timofte, and L. Van Gool, Pedestrian detection at 100 frames per second, *IEEE CVPR*, 2012. DOI: 10.1109/cvpr.2012.6248017. 45

[268] L. Zhang, B. Wu, and R. Nevatia, Pedestrian detection in infrared images based on local shape features, *IEEE CVPR Workshops*, 2007. DOI: 10.1109/CVPR.2007.383452. 45, 46

[269] R. Miezianko and D. Pokrajac, People detection in low resolution infrared videos, *IEEE CVPR Workshops*, 2008. DOI: 10.1109/cvprw.2008.4563056. 45

[270] W. Li, D. Zheng, T. Zhao, and M. Yang, An effective approach to pedestrian detection in thermal imagery, *International Conference on Natural Computation (ICNC)*, 2012. DOI: 10.1109/icnc.2012.6234621. 45, 46

[271] B. Leibe, A. Leonardis, and B. Schiele, Robust object detection with interleaved categorization and segmentation, *International Journal of Computer Vision (IJCV)*, 77(1–3):259–289, 2008. DOI: 10.1007/s11263-007-0095-3. 45

[272] P. F. Felzenszwalb, R. B. Girshick, D. McAllester, and D. Ramanan, Object detection with discriminatively trained part based models, *IEEE Transactions on Pattern Analysis and Machine Intelligence*, 32(9):1627–1645, 2010. DOI: 10.1109/tpami.2009.167. 45

[273] K. Jüngling and M. Arens, Feature based person detection beyond the visible spectrum, *IEEE CVPR Workshops*, 2009. DOI: 10.1109/CVPRW.2009.5204085. 45

[274] A. González, Z. Fang, Y. Socarras, J. Serrat, David Vázquez, J. Xu, and A. M. López, Pedestrian detection at day/night time with visible and FIR cameras: A comparison, *Sensors*, 16(6):820, Basel, Switzerland, 2016. DOI: 10.3390/s16060820. 45, 46

[275] D. König, Deep learning for person detection in multi-spectral videos, Master's Thesis, Ulm University, Ulm, Germany, 2017. 45, 46

[276] J. Wang, G. Bebis, and R. Miller, Robust video-based surveillance by integrating target detection with tracking, *IEEE CVPR Workshops*, 2006. DOI: 10.1109/CVPRW.2006.180. 45

[277] T. Elguebaly and N. Bouguila, A nonparametric Bayesian approach for enhanced pedestrian detection and foreground segmentation, *IEEE CVPR Workshops*, 2011. DOI: 10.1109/cvprw.2011.5981800. 39, 45

[278] B. Chen, W. Wang, and Q. Qin, Robust multi-stage approach for the detection of moving target from infrared imagery, *SPIE Optical Engineering*, 51(6), 2012. DOI: 10.1117/1.oe.51.6.067006. 39, 45

[279] M. Teutsch, T. Müller, M. Huber, and J. Beyerer, Low resolution person detection with a moving thermal infrared camera by hot spot classification, *IEEE CVPR Workshops*, 2014. DOI: 10.1109/cvprw.2014.40. 45, 46

[280] C. Herrmann, T. Müller, D. Willersinn, and J. Beyerer, Real-time person detection in low-resolution thermal infrared imagery with MSER and CNNs, *Proc. of SPIE*, 9987, 2016. DOI: 10.1117/12.2240940. 45

[281] M. Soga, S. Hiratsuka, H. Fukamachi, and Y. Ninomiya, Pedestrian detection for a near infrared imaging system, *IEEE International Conference on Intelligent Transportation Systems (ITSC)*, 2008. DOI: 10.1109/itsc.2008.4732710. 46

[282] J. Dong, J. Ge, and Y. Luo, Nighttime pedestrian detection with near infrared using cascaded classifiers, *IEEE ICIP*, 2007. DOI: 10.1109/icip.2007.4379552. 46

[283] Y. Lee, Y. Chan, L. Fu, P. Hsiao, L. Chuangs, Y. Chen, and M. Luo, Nighttime pedestrian detection by selecting strong near-infrared parts and enhanced spatially local model, *IEEE International Conference on Intelligent Transportation Systems (ITSC)*, 2012. DOI: 10.1109/itsc.2012.6338849. 46

[284] P. Pawlowski, K. Piniarski, and A. Dabrowski, Pedestrian detection in low resolution night vision images, *Signal Processing: Algorithms, Architectures, Arrangements, and Applications (SPA)*, 2015. DOI: 10.1109/spa.2015.7365157. 46

[285] R. Brehar, C. Vancea, and S. Nedevschi, Pedestrian detection in infrared images using aggregated channel features, *IEEE International Conference on Intelligent Computer Communication and Processing (ICCP)*, 2014. DOI: 10.1109/iccp.2014.6936964. 46

[286] T. Kim and S. Kim, Pedestrian detection at night time in FIR domain: Comprehensive study about temperature and brightness and new benchmark, *Pattern Recognition*, 79:44–54, 2018. DOI: 10.1016/j.patcog.2018.01.029. 46

[287] M. Khan, G. Fan, D. R. Heisterkamp, and L. Yu, Automatic target recognition in infrared imagery using dense hog features and relevance grouping of vocabulary, *IEEE CVPR Workshops*, 2014. DOI: 10.1109/cvprw.2014.52. 46, 62

[288] V. M. Patel, N. M. Nasrabadi, and R. Chellappa, Sparsity motivated automatic target recognition, *Applied Optics*, 50(10):1425–1433, 2011. DOI: 10.1364/ao.50.001425. 46

[289] R. Benenson, M. Omran, J. Hosang, and B. Schiele, Ten years of pedestrian detection, what have we learned?, *ECCV Workshops*, 2014. DOI: 10.1007/978-3-319-16181-5_47. 46

[290] A. Krizhevsky, I. Sutskever, and G. E. Hinton, ImageNet classification with deep convolutional neural networks, *International Conference on Neural Information Processing Systems (NIPS)*, 2012. 47

[291] K. Simonyan and A. Zisserman, Very deep convolutional networks for large-scale image recognition, *International Conference on Learning Representations (ICLR)*, 2015. 47

[292] Y. LeCun, Y. Bengio, and G. E. Hinton, Deep learning, *Nature*, 521:436–444, 2015. DOI: 10.1038/nature14539. 47

[293] I. Goodfellow, Y. Bengio, and A. Courville, *Deep Learning*, MIT Press, 2016. 47

[294] S. Ren, K. He, R. Girshick, and J. Sun, Faster R-CNN: Towards real-time object detection with region proposal networks, *IEEE Transactions on Pattern Analysis and Machine Intelligence*, 39(6):1136–1149, 2017. DOI: 10.1109/tpami.2016.2577031. 47

[295] W. Liu, D. Anguelov, D. Erhan, C. Szegedy, S. Reed, C. Fu, and A. Berg, SSD: Single shot MultiBox detector, *European Conference on Computer Vision (ECCV)*, 2016. DOI: 10.1007/978-3-319-46448-0_2. 47

[296] J. Redmon and A. Farhadi, YOLO9000: Better, faster, stronger, *IEEE CVPR*, 2017. DOI: 10.1109/cvpr.2017.690. 47

[297] J. Hosang, M. Omran, R. Benenson, and B. Schiele, Taking a deeper look at pedestrians, *IEEE CVPR*, 2015. DOI: 10.1109/cvpr.2015.7299034. 47

[298] L. Zhang, L. Lin, X. Liang, and K. He, Is faster R-CNN doing well for pedestrian detection?, *European Conference on Computer Vision (ECCV)*, 2016. DOI: 10.1007/978-3-319-46475-6_28. 47

[299] S. Zhang, R. Benenson, and B. Schiele, CityPersons: A diverse dataset for pedestrian detection, *IEEE CVPR*, 2017. DOI: 10.1109/cvpr.2017.474. 47

[300] J. Wagner, V. Fischer, M. Herman, and S. Behnke, Multispectral pedestrian detection using deep fusion convolutional neural networks, *European Symposium on Artificial Neural Networks, Computational Intelligence and Machine Learning (ESANN)*, 2016. 47, 48

[301] J. Liu, S. Zhang, S. Wang, and D. N. Metaxas, Multispectral deep neural networks for pedestrian detection, *British Machine Vision Conference (BMVC)*, 2016. DOI: 10.5244/c.30.73. 47, 48

[302] D. König, M. Adam, C. Jarvers, G. Layher, H. Neumann, and M. Teutsch, Fully convolutional region proposal networks for multispectral person detection, *IEEE CVPR Workshops*, 2017. DOI: 10.1109/cvprw.2017.36. 47, 48

[303] C. Herrmann, M. Ruf, and J. Beyerer, CNN-based thermal infrared person detection by domain adaptation, *Proc. of SPIE*, 10643, 2018. DOI: 10.1117/12.2304400. 47, 48

[304] K. Fritz, D. König, U. Klauck, and M. Teutsch, Generalization ability of region proposal networks for multispectral person detection, *Proc. of SPIE*, 10988, 2019. DOI: 10.1117/12.2520705. 47

[305] I. Hasan, S. Liao, J. Li, S. U. Akram, and L. Shao, Generalizable pedestrian detection: The elephant in the room, *IEEE CVPR*, 2021. 48

[306] T. Guo, C. P. Huynh, and M. Solh, Domain-adaptive pedestrian detection in thermal images, *International Conference on Image Processing (ICIP)*, 2019. DOI: 10.1109/icip.2019.8803104. 48

[307] D. Xu, W. Ouyang, E. Ricci, X. Wang, and N. Sebe, Learning cross-modal deep representations for robust pedestrian detection, *IEEE CVPR*, 2017. DOI: 10.1109/cvpr.2017.451. 48, 58, 74

[308] C. Li, D. Song, R. Tong, and M. Tang, Multispectral pedestrian detection via simultaneous detection and segmentation, *British Machine Vision Conference (BMVC)*, 2018. 48

[309] L. Zhang, X. Zhu, X. Chen, X. Yang, Z. Lei, and Z. Liu, Weakly aligned cross-modal learning for multispectral pedestrian detection, *IEEE International Conference on Computer Vision (ICCV)*, 2019. DOI: 10.1109/iccv.2019.00523. 48

[310] D. Guan, Y. Cao, J. Yang, Y. Cao, and M. Ying Yang, Fusion of multispectral data through illumination-aware deep neural networks for pedestrian detection, *Information Fusion*, 50:148–157, 2019. DOI: 10.1016/j.inffus.2018.11.017. 48

[311] C. Li, D. Song, R. Tong, and M. Tang, Illumination-aware faster R-CNN for robust multispectral pedestrian detection, *Pattern Recognition*, 85:161–171, 2019. DOI: 10.1016/j.patcog.2018.08.005. 48

[312] K. Zhou, L. Chen, and X. Cao, Improving multispectral pedestrian detection by addressing modality imbalance problems, *European Conference on Vision Conference (ECCV)*, 2020. DOI: 10.1007/978-3-030-58523-5_46. 48, 74

[313] A. Wolpert, M. Teutsch, S. Sarfraz, and R. Stiefelhagen, Anchor-free small-scale multispectral pedestrian detection, *British Machine Vision Conference (BMVC)*, 2020. 48

[314] D. Ghose, S. M. Desai, S. Bhattacharya, D. Chakraborty, M. Fiterau, and T. Rahman, Pedestrian detection in thermal images using saliency maps, *IEEE CVPR Workshops*, 2019. DOI: 10.1109/cvprw.2019.00130. 48

[315] C. Devaguptapu, N. Akolekar, M. M. Sharma, and V. N. Balasubramanian, Borrow from anywhere: Pseudo multi-modal object detection in thermal imagery, *IEEE CVPR Workshops*, 2019. DOI: 10.1109/cvprw.2019.00135. 48

[316] E. Maggio and A. Cavallaro, *Video Tracking: Theory and Practice*, Wiley, 2011. DOI: 10.1002/9780470974377. 48

[317] S. Blackman and R. Popoli *Design and Analysis of Modern Tracking Systems*, Artech House Inc., 1999. 48

[318] S. Chen, Kalman filter for robot vision: A survey, *IEEE Transactions on Industrial Electronics*, 59(11):4409–4420, 2012. DOI: 10.1109/tie.2011.2162714. 49

[319] A. Fossati, P. Schönmann, and P. Fua, Real-time vehicle tracking for driving assistance, *Machine Vision and Applications*, 22(2):439–448, 2011. DOI: 10.1007/s00138-009-0243-6. 49

[320] W. Hu, N. Xie, L. Li, X. Zeng, and S. Maybank, A survey on visual content-based video indexing and retrieval, *IEEE Transactions on Systems, Man, and Cybernetics*, 41(6):797–819, 2011. DOI: 10.1109/tsmcc.2011.2109710. 49

[321] S. Mitra and T. Acharya, Gesture recognition: A survey, *IEEE Transactions on Systems, Man, and Cybernetics*, 37(3):311–324, 2007. DOI: 10.1109/tsmcc.2007.893280. 49

[322] A. Yilmaz, O. Javed, and M. Shah, Object tracking: A survey, *ACM Computing Surveys (CSUR)*, 38(4), 2006. DOI: 10.1145/1177352.1177355. 49

[323] K. Bernardin and R. Stiefelhagen, Evaluating multiple object tracking performance: The CLEAR MOT metrics, *EURASIP Journal on Image and Video Processing*, 2008. DOI: 10.1155/2008/246309. 50

[324] B. Karasulu and S. Korukoglu, A software for performance evaluation and comparison of people detection and tracking methods in video processing, *MTA*, 55(3):677–723, 2011. DOI: 10.1007/s11042-010-0591-2. 50

[325] A. Sanin, C. Sanderson, and B. C. Lovell, Shadow detection: A survey and comparative evaluation of recent methods, *Pattern Recognition*, 45(4):1684–1695, 2012. DOI: 10.1016/j.patcog.2011.10.001. 50

[326] A. Smeulders, D. Chu, R. Cucchiara, S. Calderara, A. Dehghan, and M. Shah, Visual tracking: An experimental survey, *IEEE Transactions on Pattern Analysis and Machine Intelligence*, 36(7):1442–1468, 2014. DOI: 10.1109/tpami.2013.230. 50, 53

[327] M. Kristan, J. Matas, A. Leonardis, T. Vojir, R. Pflugfelder, G. Fernandez, G. Nebehay, F. Porikli, and L, Čehovin, A novel performance evaluation methodology for single-target trackers, *IEEE Transactions on Pattern Analysis and Machine Intelligence*, 38(11):2137–2155, 2016. DOI: 10.1109/tpami.2016.2516982. 50

[328] Y. Wu, J. Lim, and M.-H. Yang, Object tracking benchmark, *IEEE Transactions on Pattern Analysis and Machine Intelligence*, 37(9):1834–1848, 2015. DOI: 10.1109/tpami.2014.2388226. 50

[329] H. Fan, L. Lin, F. Yang, P. Chu, G. Deng, S. Yu, H. Bai, Y. Xu, C. Liao, and H. Ling, LaSOT: A high-quality benchmark for large-scale single object tracking, *IEEE CVPR*, 2019. DOI: 10.1109/cvpr.2019.00552. 50

[330] M. Müller, N. Smith, and B. Ghanem, A benchmark and simulator for UAV tracking, *European Conference on Computer Vision (ECCV)*, 2016. DOI: 10.1007/978-3-319-46448-0_27. 50

[331] P. Bergmann, T. Meinhardt, and L. Leal-Taixe, Tracking without bells and whistles, *IEEE ICCV*, 2019. DOI: 10.1109/iccv.2019.00103. 50

[332] Y. Bar-Shalom and T. E. Fortmann, *Tracking and Data Association*, Elsevier Science Publishing, 1988. 50

[333] H. W. Kuhn, The Hungarian method for solving the assignment problem, *Naval Research Logistics Quarterly*, 2:83–97, 1955. DOI: 10.1002/nav.3800020109. 50

[334] G. A. Mills-Tettey, A. Stentz, and M. B. Dias, The dynamic Hungarian algorithm for the assignment problem with changing costs, *Technical Report*, Carnegie Mellon University, Pittsburgh, 2007. 50

[335] I. Saleemi and M. Shah, Multiframe many-many point correspondence for tracking of swarms of vehicles in wide area aerial videos, *International Journal of Computer Vision (IJCV)*, 104(2):198–219, 2013. DOI: 10.1007/s11263-013-0624-1. 50

[336] A. G. A. Perera, C. Srinivas, A. Hoogs, G. Brooksby, and W. Hu, Multi-object tracking through simultaneous long occlusions and split-merge conditions, *IEEE CVPR*, 2006. DOI: 10.1109/cvpr.2006.195. 38, 50

[337] J. F. Henriques, R. Caseiro, and J. Batista, Globally optimal solution to multi-object tracking with merged measurements, *IEEE International Conference on Computer Vision (ICCV*, 2011. DOI: 10.1109/iccv.2011.6126532. 50

[338] B. Wu and R. Nevatia, Tracking of multiple, partially occluded humans based on static body part detection, *IEEE CVPR*, 2006. DOI: 10.1109/cvpr.2006.312. 50

[339] A. Milan, K. Schindler, and S. Roth, Challenges of ground truth evaluation of multi-target tracking, *IEEE CVPR Workshops*, 2013. DOI: 10.1109/cvprw.2013.111. 50

[340] W. Luo, J. Xing, A. Milan, X. Zhang, W. Liu, X. Zhao, and T. Kim, Multiple object tracking: A literature review, *ArXiv:1409.7618*, 2017. DOI: 10.1016/j.artint.2020.103448. 50

[341] L. Leal-Taixé, A. Milan, I. Reid, S. Roth, and K. Schindler, MOTChallenge 2015: Towards a benchmark for multi-target tracking, *ArXiv:1504.01942*, 2015. 50

[342] A. Milan, L. Leal-Taixé, I. Reid, S. Roth, and K. Schindler, MOT16: A benchmark for multi-object tracking, *ArXiv:1603.00831*, 2016. 50

[343] Q. Liu and Z. He, PTB-TIR: A thermal infrared pedestrian tracking benchmark, *ArXiv:1801.05944*, 2018. DOI: 10.1109/tmm.2019.2932615. 51

[344] M. Felsberg et al., The thermal infrared visual object tracking VOT-TIR2016 challenge results, *European Conference on Computer Vision Workshops (ECCVW)*, 2016. DOI: 10.1007/978-3-319-48881-3_55. 51, 52

[345] M. Kristan et al., The eighth visual object tracking VOT2020 challenge results, *European Conference on Computer Vision Workshops (ECCVW)*, 2020. DOI: 10.1007/978-3-030-68238-5_39. 52

[346] A. Berg, J. Ahlberg, and M. Felsberg, A thermal object tracking benchmark, *IEEE Internation Conference Advanced Video and Signal Based Surveillance (AVSS)*, 2015. DOI: 10.1109/avss.2015.7301772. 51, 52

[347] M. Felsberg et al., The thermal infrared visual object tracking VOT-TIR2015 challenge results, *IEEE International Conference on Computer Vision Workshops (ICCVW)*, 2015. DOI: 10.1109/iccvw.2015.86. 52

[348] Z. Wu, N. Fuller, D. Theriault, and M. Betke, A thermal infrared video benchmark for visual analysis, *IEEE CVPR Workshops*, 2014. DOI: 10.1109/cvprw.2014.39. 51, 52

[349] Q. Liu et al., LSOTB-TIR: A large-scale high-diversity thermal infrared object tracking benchmark, *ACM International Conference on Multimedia (MM)*, 2020. DOI: 10.1145/3394171.3413922. 51, 52, 53, 79

[350] C. Li, H. Cheng, S. Hu, X. Liu, J. Tang, and L. Lin, Learning collaborative sparse representation for grayscale-thermal tracking, *IEEE Transactions on Image Processing*, 25(12):5743–5756, 2016. DOI: 10.1109/tip.2016.2614135. 51, 52, 54

[351] P.-L. St-Charles, G.-A. Bilodeau, and R. Bergevin, Mutual foreground segmentation with multispectral stereo pairs, *IEEE International Conference on Computer Vision Workshops (ICCVW)*, 2017. DOI: 10.1109/iccvw.2017.55. 52

[352] E. Bondi et al., BIRDSAI: A dataset for detection and tracking in aerial thermal infrared videos, *IEEE Winter Conference on Applications in Computer Vision (WACV)*, 2020. DOI: 10.1109/wacv45572.2020.9093284. 51, 52

[353] K. Briechle and U. D. Hanebeck, Template matching using fast normalized cross correlation, *Proc. of SPIE*, 4387, 2001. DOI: 10.1117/12.421129. 53

[354] D. Comaniciu, V. Ramesh, and P. Meer, Real-time tracking of non-rigid objects using mean shift, *IEEE CVPR*, 2000. DOI: 10.1109/cvpr.2000.854761. 53

[355] X. Mei and H. Ling, Robust visual tracking using L1 minimization, *IEEE International Conference on Computer Vision (ICCV)*, 2009. DOI: 10.1109/ICCV.2009.5459292. 53

[356] B. Babenko, M.-H. Yang, and S. Belongie, Visual tracking with online multiple instance learning, *IEEE CVPR*, 2009. DOI: 10.1109/cvpr.2009.5206737. 53

[357] S. Hare, A. Saffari, and P. H. S. Torr, Struck: Structured output tracking with kernels, *IEEE International Conference on Computer Vision (ICCV)*, 2011. DOI: 10.1109/iccv.2011.6126251. 53

[358] J. F. Henriques, R. Caseiro, P. Martins, and J. Batista, High-speed tracking with kernelized correlation filters, *IEEE Transactions on Pattern Analysis and Machine Intelligence*, 37(3):583–596, 2015. DOI: 10.1109/tpami.2014.2345390. 53

[359] M. Tang and J. Feng, Multi-kernel correlation filter for visual tracking, *IEEE CVPR*, 2015. DOI: 10.1109/iccv.2015.348. 53, 55

[360] M. Danelljan, G. Bhat, F. Shahbaz Khan, and M. Felsberg, Eco: Efficient convolution operators for tracking, *IEEE CVPR*, 2017. DOI: 10.1109/cvpr.2017.733. 53

[361] L. Bertinetto, J. Valmadre, J. F. Henriques, A. Vedaldi, and P. H. Torr, Fully-convolutional siamese networks for object tracking, *European Conference on Computer Vision Workshops (ECCVW)*, 2016. DOI: 10.1007/978-3-319-48881-3_56. 53

[362] A. He, C. Luo, X. Tian, and W. Zeng, A twofold siamese network for real-time object tracking, *IEEE CVPR*, 2018. DOI: 10.1109/cvpr.2018.00508. 53

[363] F. Zhou, W. Chen, and H. Fang, Robust eye tracking and location method based on Particle filtering algorithm, *IEEE International Conference on Cloud Computing and Intelligence Systems*, 2014. DOI: 10.1109/ccis.2014.7175737. 54

[364] J. Wu, W. Ou, and C. Fan, NIR-based gaze tracking with fast pupil ellipse fitting for real-time wearable eye trackers, *IEEE Conference on Dependable and Secure Computing*, 2017. DOI: 10.1109/desec.2017.8073839. 54

[365] M. S. Willers and C. J. Willers, Key considerations in infrared simulations of the missile-aircraft engagement, *Proc. of SPIE*, 8543, 2012. DOI: 10.1117/12.974801. 54

[366] G. A. Tidhar, O. B. Aphek, and E. Cohen, OTHELLO: A novel SWIR dual-band detection system and its applications, *Proc. of SPIE*, 8704, 2013. DOI: 10.1117/12.2019202. 54

[367] E. Gundogdu, H. Ozkan, H. S. Demir, H. Ergezer, E. Akagündüz, and S. K. Pakin, Comparison of infrared and visible imagery for object tracking: Toward trackers with superior IR performance, *IEEE CVPR Workshops*, 2015. DOI: 10.1109/cvprw.2015.7301290. 54

[368] A. Berg, J. Ahlberg, and M. Felsberg, Channel coded distribution field tracking for thermal infrared imagery, *IEEE CVPR Workshops*, 2016. DOI: 10.1109/cvprw.2016.158. 54

[369] D. S. Bolme, J. R. Beveridge, B. A. Draper, and Y. M. Lui, Visual object tracking using adaptive correlation filters, *IEEE CVPR*, 2010. DOI: 10.1109/cvpr.2010.5539960. 54

[370] L. Sevilla-Lara and E. G. Learned-Miller, Distribution fields for tracking, *IEEE CVPR*, 2012. DOI: 10.1109/cvpr.2012.6247891. 54

[371] M. Felsberg, Enhanced distribution field tracking using channel representations, *IEEE International Conference on Computer Vision (ICCV) Workshops*, 2013. DOI: 10.1109/iccvw.2013.22. 54

[372] E. Gundogdu, A. Koc, B. Solmaz, R. I. Hammoud, and A. A. Alatan, Evaluation of feature channels for correlation-filter-based visual object tracking in infrared spectrum, *IEEE CVPR Workshops*, 2016. DOI: 10.1109/cvprw.2016.43. 55

[373] Q. Liu, X. Lu, Z. He, C. Zhang, and W. S. Chen, Deep convolutional neural networks for thermal infrared object tracking, *Knowledge-Based Systems*, 134:189–198, 2017. DOI: 10.1016/j.knosys.2017.07.032. 55

[374] L. Zhang, A. Gonzalez-Garcia, J. van de Weijer, M. Danelljan, and F. S. Khan, Synthetic data generation for end-to-end thermal infrared tracking, *IEEE Transactions on Image Processing*, 28(4):1837–1850, 2019. DOI: 10.1109/tip.2018.2879249. 55, 79

[375] Q. Liu, X. Li, Z. He, N. Fan, D. Yuan, W. Liu, and Y. Liang, Multi-task driven feature model for thermal infrared tracking, *AAAI Conference on Artificial Intelligence*, 2020. 55

[376] X. Li, Q. Liu, N. Fan, Z. He, and H. Wang, Hierarchical spatial-aware Siamese network for thermal infrared object tracking, *Knowledge-Based Systems*, 166:71–81, 2019. DOI: 10.1016/j.knosys.2018.12.011. 55

[377] Q. Liu, X. Li, Z. He, N. Fan, D. Yuan, and H. Wang, Learning deep multi-level similarity for thermal infrared object tracking, *IEEE Transactions on Multimedia*, Early Access, 2020. DOI: 10.1109/tmm.2020.3008028. 55

[378] L. Zhang, M. Danelljan, A. Gonzalez-Garcia, J. van de Weijer, and F. S. Khan, Multimodal fusion for end-to-end RGB-T tracking, *IEEE ICCV Workshops*, 2019. DOI: 10.1109/iccvw.2019.00278. 56

[379] P. Zhang, J. Zhao, D. Wang, H. Lu, and X. Yang, Jointly modeling motion and appearance cues for robust RGB-T tracking, *IEEE Transactions on Image Processing*, 30:3335–3347, 2021. DOI: 10.1109/tip.2021.3060862. 56

[380] C. Padole and L. Alexandre, Wigner distribution-based motion tracking of human beings using thermal imaging, *IEEE CVPR Workshops*, 2010. DOI: 10.1109/cvprw.2010.5543226. 56

[381] F. Lamberti, A. Sanna, and G. Paravati, Improving robustness of infrared target tracking algorithms based on template matching, *IEEE Transactions on Aerospace and Electronic Systems*, 47(2):1467–1480, 2011. DOI: 10.1109/taes.2011.5751271. 56

[382] K. Jüngling and M. Arens, Pedestrian tracking in infrared from moving vehicles, *IEEE Intelligent Vehicles Symposium (IV)*, 2010. DOI: 10.1109/ivs.2010.5548132. 56

[383] S. Lee, G. Shah, A. Bhattacharya, and Y. Motai, Human tracking with an infrared camera using a curve matching framework, *EURASIP Journal on Advances in Signal Processing*, 2012(1), 2012. DOI: 10.1186/1687-6180-2012-99. 56

[384] R. Hammoud, G. Fan, R. W. McMillan, and K. Ikeuchi (Eds.), *Machine Vision Beyond Visible Spectrum*, Springer, 2011. DOI: 10.1007/978-3-642-11568-4. 56

[385] V. Badrinarayanan, A. Kendall, and R. Cipolla, SegNet: A deep convolutional encoder-decoder architecture for image segmentation, *IEEE Transactions on Pattern Analysis and Machine Intelligence*, 39(12):2481–2495, 2017. DOI: 10.1109/tpami.2016.2644615. 56, 57

[386] J. Wang, K. Sun, T. Cheng, et al., Deep high-resolution representation learning for visual recognition, *IEEE Transactions on Pattern Analysis and Machine Intelligence*, Early Access, 2019. DOI: 10.1109/tpami.2020.2983686. 56

[387] F. Schroff, A. Criminisi, and A. Zisserman, Object class segmentation using random forests, *British Machine Vision Conference (BMVC)*, 2008. DOI: 10.5244/c.22.54. 56

[388] M. Cordts, M. Omran, S. Ramos, T. Rehfeld, M. Enzweiler, R. Benenson, U. Franke, S. Roth, and B. Schiele, The cityscapes dataset for semantic urban scene understanding, *IEEE CVPR*, 2016. DOI: 10.1109/cvpr.2016.350. 56

[389] O. Ronneberger, P. Fischer, and T. Brox, U-Net: Convolutional networks for biomedical image segmentation, *Medical Image Computing and Computer-Assisted Intervention (MIC-CAI)*, Springer LNCS, 9351:234–241, 2015. DOI: 10.1007/978-3-319-24574-4_28. 56

[390] B. H. Menze, A. Jakab, S. Bauer, et al., The multimodal brain tumor image segmentation benchmark (BRATS), *IEEE Transactions on Medical Imaging*, 34(10):1993–2024, 2015. DOI: 10.1109/TMI.2014.2377694. 56

[391] C. Li, W. Xia, Y. Yan, B. Luo, and J. Tang, Segmenting objects in day and night: Edge-conditioned CNN for thermal image semantic segmentation, *IEEE Transactions on Neural Networks and Learning Systems*, Early Access, 2020. DOI: 10.1109/tnnls.2020.3009373. 57

[392] Y. Zang, B. Yu, L. Yu, D. Yang, and Q. Liu, Far-infrared object segmentation focus on transmission of overall semantic information, *IEEE Access*, 8:182564–182579, 2020. DOI: 10.1109/access.2020.3028656. 57

[393] Q. Ha, K. Watanabe, T. Karasawa, Y. Ushiku, and T. Harada, MFNet: Towards real-time semantic segmentation for autonomous vehicles with multi-spectral scenes, *IEEE/RSJ International Conference on Intelligent Robots and Systems (IROS)*, 2017. DOI: 10.1109/iros.2017.8206396. 57

[394] Y. Sun, W. Zuo, P. Yun, H. Wang, and M. Liu, FuseSeg: Semantic segmentation of urban scenes based on RGB and thermal data fusion, *IEEE Transactions on Automation Science and Engineering*, Early Access, 2020. DOI: 10.1109/tase.2020.2993143. 57

[395] R. Brehar, F. Vancea, T. Marița, and S. Nedevschi, A deep learning approach for pedestrian segmentation in infrared images, *IEEE International Conference on Intelligent Computer Communication and Processing (ICCP)*, 2018. DOI: 10.1109/iccp.2018.8516630. 57

[396] P. Wang and X. Bai, Thermal infrared pedestrian segmentation based on conditional GAN, *IEEE Transactions on Image Processing*, 28(12):6007–6021, 2019. DOI: 10.1109/tip.2019.2924171. 57

[397] S. Vishwakarma and A. Agrawa, A survey on activity recognition and behavior understanding in video surveillance, *The Visual Computer*, 29(10), 2012. DOI: 10.1007/s00371-012-0752-6. 57

[398] G. Varol, I. Laptev, and C. Schmid, Long-term temporal convolutions for action recognition, *IEEE Transactions on Pattern Analysis and Machine Intelligence*, 40(6):1510–1517, 2018. DOI: 10.1109/tpami.2017.2712608. 57

[399] D. Weinland, R. Ronfard, and E. Boyer, A survey of vision-based methods for action representation, segmentation and recognition, *Computer Vision and Image Understanding (CVIU)*, 115(2):224–241, 2011. DOI: 10.1016/j.cviu.2010.10.002. 57

[400] S. Herath, M. Harandi, and F. Porikli, Going deeper into action recognition: A survey, *Image and Vision Computing (IVC)*, 60:4–21, 2017. DOI: 10.1016/j.imavis.2017.01.010. 57

[401] H. Alwassel, F. Heilbron, and B. Ghanem, Action search: Spotting actions in videos and its application to temporal action localization, *European Conference on Computer Vision (ECCV)*, 2018. DOI: 10.1007/978-3-030-01240-3_16. 57

[402] S. Ali and M. Shah, Human action recognition in videos using kinematic features and multiple instance learning, *IEEE Transactions on Pattern Analysis and Machine Intelligence*, 32(2):288–303, 2010. DOI: 10.1109/tpami.2008.284. 57

[403] H. Rahmani, A. Mian, and M. Shah, Learning a deep model for human action recognition from novel viewpoints, *IEEE Transactions on Pattern Analysis and Machine Intelligence*, 40(3):667–681, 2018. DOI: 10.1109/tpami.2017.2691768. 57

[404] S. Ali and N. Bouguila, Variational learning of beta-liouville hidden Markov models for infrared action recognition, *IEEE CVPR Workshops*, 2019. DOI: 10.1109/cvprw.2019.00119. 57, 58

[405] J. Li and W. Gong, Application of thermal infrared imagery in human action recognition, *Advanced Materials Research*, 121–222:368–372, 2010. DOI: 10.4028/www.scientific.net/amr.121-122.368. 58

[406] A. Bobick and J. W. Davis, The recognition of human movement using temporal templates, *IEEE Transactions on Pattern Analysis and Machine Intelligence*, 23(3):257–267, 2001. DOI: 10.1109/34.910878. 58

[407] Z. Jiang, V. Rozgic, and S. Adali, Learning spatiotemporal features for infrared action recognition with 3D convolutional neural networks, *IEEE CVPR Workshops*, 2017. DOI: 10.1109/cvprw.2017.44. 58

[408] M. de la Riva and P. Mettes, Bayesian 3D ConvNets for action recognition from few examples, *IEEE ICCV Workshops*, 2019. DOI: 10.1109/iccvw.2019.00169. 58

[409] Y. Liu, Z. Lu, J. Li, T. Yang, and C. Yao, Global temporal representation based CNNs for infrared action recognition, *IEEE Signal Processing Letters*, 25(6):848–852, 2018. DOI: 10.1109/lsp.2018.2823910. 58

[410] J. Imran and B. Raman, Deep residual infrared action recognition by integrating local and global spatio-temporal cues, *Infrared Physics and Technology*, 102, 2019. DOI: 10.1016/j.infrared.2019.103014. 58

[411] Y. Zhu and G. Guo, A study on visible to infrared action recognition, *IEEE Signal Processing Letters*, 20(9):897–900, 2013. DOI: 10.1109/lsp.2013.2272920. 58

[412] L. Wang, C. Gao, L. Yang, Y. Zhao, W. Zuo, and D. Meng, PM-GANs: Discriminative representation learning for action recognition using partial-modalities, *ECCV*, 2018. DOI: 10.1007/978-3-030-01231-1_24. 58

[413] C. Gao, Y. Du, J. Liu, J. Lv, L. Yang, D. Meng, and A. Hauptmann, Infar dataset: Infrared action recognition at different times, *Neurocomputing*, 212:36–47, 2016. DOI: 10.1016/j.neucom.2016.05.094. 58

[414] S. Oh et al., A large-scale benchmark dataset for even recognition in surveillance video, *IEEE CVPR*, 2011. DOI: 10.1109/CVPR.2011.5995586. 58, 60, 62, 63

[415] M. Vandersteegen, W. Reusen, K. Van Beeck, and T. Goedemé, Low-latency hand gesture recognition with a low resolution thermal imager, *IEEE CVPR Workshops*, 2020. DOI: 10.1109/cvprw50498.2020.00057. 58

[416] M. Cokbas, P. Ishwar, and J. Konrad, Low-resolution overhead thermal tripwire for occupancy estimation, *IEEE CVPR Workshops*, 2020. DOI: 10.1109/cvprw50498.2020.00052. 58

[417] L. Wang, G. Leedham, and D. S-Y. Cho, Minutiae feature analysis for infrared hand vein pattern biometrics, *Pattern Recognition*, 41(3):920–929, 2008. DOI: 10.1016/j.patcog.2007.07.012. 58

[418] P. Gupta and P. Gupta, Multibiometric authentication system using slap fingerprints, palm dorsal vein, and hand geometry, *IEEE Transactions on Industrial Electronics*, 65(12):9777–9784, 2018. DOI: 10.1109/tie.2018.2823686. 58

[419] M. Diakides, J. D. Bronzino, and D. R. Peterson, *Medial Infrared Imaging: Principles and Practices*, CRC Press, 2012. 58

[420] S. Ariffin, N. Jamil, and P. Rahman, DIAST variability illuminated thermal and visible ear images datasets, *Signal Processing: Algorithms, Architectures, Arrangements, and Applications (SPA)*, 2016. DOI: 10.1109/spa.2016.7763611. 58

[421] J. Bader, B. Labitzke, M. Grzegorzek, and A. Kolb, Multispectral pattern recognition techniques for biometrics, *Technical Report*, Siegen University, Siegen, Germany, 2011. 58

[422] J. Liu et al., NTIRE 2021 multi-modal aerial view object classification challenge, *IEEE CVPR Workshops*, 2021. DOI: 10.1109/cvprw53098.2021.00071. 59

[423] C. L. P. Chen, H. Li, Y. Wei, T. Xia, and Y. Y. Tang, A local contrast method for small infrared target detection, *IEEE Transactions on Geoscience and Remote Sensing*, 52(1):574–581, 2014. DOI: 10.1109/tgrs.2013.2242477. 60

[424] H. Deng, X. Sun, M. Liu, C. Ye, and X. Zhou, Small infrared target detection based on weighted local difference measure, *IEEE Transactions on Geoscience and Remote Sensing*, 54(7):4204–4214, 2016. DOI: 10.1109/tgrs.2016.2538295. 60

[425] Y. Dai and Y. Wu, Reweighted infrared patch-tensor model with both non-local and local priors for single-frame small target detection, *IEEE Journal of Selected Topics in Applied Earth Observations and Remote Sensing*, 10(8):3752–3767, 2017. DOI: 10.1109/jstars.2017.2700023. 60

[426] M. Fan, S. Tian, K. Liu, J. Zhao, and Y. Li, Infrared small target detection based on region proposal and CNN classifier, *Signal, Image and Video Processing*, Springer, 2021. DOI: 10.1007/s11760-021-01936-z. 60

[427] Y. Dai, Y. Wu, F. Zhou, and K. Barnard, Asymmetric contextual modulation for infrared small target detection, *IEEE Winter Conference on Applications of Computer Vision (WACV)*, 2021. DOI: 10.1109/wacv48630.2021.00099. 60

[428] R. I. Hammoud (Ed.), *Augmented Vision Perception in Infrared: Algorithms and Applied Systems*, Springer, 2009. 62

[429] F. Sadjadi and B. Javidi (Eds.), *Physics of Automatic Target Recognition*, Springer, 2007. 62

[430] L. Yu, G. Fan, J. Gong, and J. Havlicek, Joint infrared target recognition and segmentation using a shape manifold-aware level set, *Sensors*, 15(5):10118–10145, 2015. DOI: 10.3390/s150510118. 62

[431] V. Venkataraman, G. Fan, L. Yu, X. Zhang, W. Liu, and J. Havlicek, Automated target tracking and recognition using coupled view and identity manifolds for shape representation, *EURASIP Journal on Advances in Signal Processing*, 2011(24), 2011. DOI: 10.1186/1687-6180-2011-124. 62

[432] A. d'Acremont, R. Fablet, A. Baussard, and G. Quin, CNN-based target recognition and identification for infrared imaging in defense systems, *Sensors*, 19(9), 2019. DOI: 10.3390/s19092040. 62

[433] R. I. Hammoud, D. S. Pineo, and W. Snyder, Performance analysis of deep learning-based automatic target recognition, *Proc. of SPIE*, 10648, 2018. DOI: 10.1117/12.2315374. 62

[434] J. Gong, G. Fan, L. Yu, J. P. Havlicek, D. Chen, and N. Fan, Joint target tracking, recognition and segmentation for infrared imagery using a shape manifold-based level set, *Sensors*, 14(6):10124–10145, 2014. DOI: 10.3390/s140610124. 62

[435] R. I. Hammoud, C. S. Sahin, E. Blasch, B. J. Rhodes, and T. Wang, Automatic association of chats and video tracks for activity learning and recognition in aerial video surveillance, *Sensors*, 14(10):19843–19860, 2014. DOI: 10.3390/s141019843. 62

[436] D. Garagic, J. Peskoe, F. Liu, M. Cuevas, A. M. Freeman, and B. J. Rhodes, Long-range dismount activity classification: LODAC, *Proc. of SPIE* 9079, 2014. DOI: 10.1117/12.2053090. 62

[437] A. Hoogs et al., An end-to-end system for content-based video retrieval using behavior, actions, and appearance with interactive query refinement, *IEEE International Conference on Advanced Video and Signal-based Surveillance (AVSS)*, 2015. DOI: 10.1109/avss.2015.7301807. 62

[438] J. Zhu, O. Javed, J. Liu, and Q. Yu, Pedestrian detection in low-resolution imagery by learning multi-scale intrinsic motion structures (MIMS), *IEEE CVPR*, 2014. DOI: 10.1109/cvpr.2014.449. 62

[439] J. Prokaj, Exploitation of Wide Area Motion Imagery, Dissertation, University of Southern California, Los Angeles, CA, 2013. 63

[440] A. Basharat et al., Real-time multi-target tracking at 210 megapixels/second in wide area motion imageryn, *IEEE Winter Conference on Applied Computer Vision (WACV)*, 2014. DOI: 10.1109/wacv.2014.6836016. 63

[441] R. LaLonde, D. Zhang, and M. Shah, ClusterNet: Detecting small objects in large scenes by exploiting spatio-temporal information, *IEEE CVPR*, 2018. DOI: 10.1109/cvpr.2018.00421. 63

[442] L. Sommer, W. Krüger, and M. Teutsch, Appearance and motion-based persistent multiple object tracking in wide area motion imagery, *IEEE ICCV Workshops*, 2021. 63

[443] J. Gao, H. Ling, E. Blasch, K. Pham, Z. Wang, and G. Chen Pattern of life from WAMI objects tracking based on context-aware tracking and information network models, *Proc. of SPIE*, 8745, 2013. 63

[444] L. Patino, T. Nawaz, T. Cane, and J. Ferryman, PETS 2017: Dataset and challenge, *IEEE CVPR Workshops*, 2017. DOI: 10.1109/cvprw.2017.264. 63

[445] E. Ristani, F. Solera, R. Zou, R. Cucchiara, and C. Tomasi, Performance measures and a data set for multi-target, multi-camera tracking, *ECCV Workshops*, 2016. DOI: 10.1007/978-3-319-48881-3_2. 63

[446] J. R. Padilla-Lopez, A. A. Chaaraoui, and F. Florez-Revuelta, Visual privacy protection methods: A survey, *Expert Systems with Applications*, 42(9):4177–4195, 2015. DOI: 10.1016/j.eswa.2015.01.041. 64

[447] M. Kieu, A. D. Bagdanov, M. Bertini, and A. del Bimbo, Task-conditioned domain adaptation for pedestrian detection in thermal imagery, *International Conference on Image Analysis and Processing (ICIAP)*, 2019. DOI: 10.1007/978-3-030-58542-6_33. 64

[448] B. Göhler and P. Lutzmann, Penetration of pyrotechnic effects with SWIR laser gated viewing in comparison to VIS and thermal IR bands, *Proc. of SPIE* 9988, 2016. DOI: 10.1117/12.2241072. 66

[449] A. K. Jain, P. Flynn, and A. A. Ross (Eds.), *Handbook of Biometrics*, Springer, 2008. DOI: 10.1007/978-0-387-71041-9. 66

[450] N. V. Boulgouris, K. N. Plataniotis, and E. Micheli-Tzanakou (Eds.), *Biometrics—Theory, Methods, and Applications*, Wiley, 2009. DOI: 10.5962/bhl.title.61967. 66

[451] J. Kang, Face recognition for vehicle personalization, Dissertation, Georgia Institute of Technology, 2016. 66

[452] A. K. Jain and A. A. Ross, Bridging the gap: From biometrics to forensics, *Philosophical Transactions of the Royal Society B*, 370(1674), 2015. DOI: 10.1098/rstb.2014.0254. 66

[453] J. Neves, F. Narducci, S. Barra, and H. Proenca, Biometric recognition in surveillance scenarios: A survey, *Artificial Intelligence Review*, 46(4):515–541, 2016. DOI: 10.1007/s10462-016-9474-x. 66

[454] U. Konuk, Infrared face recognition, Master's Thesis, Middle East Technical University, Turkey, 2015. 66, 68, 71

[455] X. Sun, L. Huang, and C. Liu, Context based face spoofing detection using active near-infrared images, *International Conference on Pattern Recognition (ICPR)*, 2016. DOI: 10.1109/icpr.2016.7900303. 66

[456] M. Wimmer, B. A. MacDonald, D. Jayamuni, and A. Yadav, Facial expression recognition for human-robot interaction—a prototype, *International Workshop on Robot Vision (RobVis)*, 2008. DOI: 10.1007/978-3-540-78157-8_11. 66

[457] L. A. Jeni, H. Hashimoto, and T. Kubota, Robust facial expression recognition using near infrared cameras, *Journal of Advanced Computational Intelligence and Intelligent Informatics*, 16(2):341–348, 2012. DOI: 10.20965/jaciii.2012.p0341. 66

[458] E. Murphy-Chutorian, A. Doshi, and M. M. Trivedi, Head pose estimation for driver assistance systems: A robust algorithm and experimental evaluation, *IEEE Intelligent Transportation Systems Conference (ITSC)*, 2007. DOI: 10.1109/itsc.2007.4357803. 66

[459] H. C. Kim, J. Cha, and W. D. Lee, Eye detection for near infrared-based gaze tracking system, *International Conference on Information Science and Applications (ICISA)*, 2014. DOI: 10.1109/icisa.2014.6847398. 66

[460] P. Chynal and J. Sobecki, Application of thermal imaging camera in eye tracking evaluation, *International Conference on Human System Interactions (HSI)*, 2016. DOI: 10.1109/hsi.2016.7529673. 66

[461] A. Nech and I. Kemelmacher-Shlizerman, Level playing field for million scale face recognition, *IEEE CVPR*, 2017. DOI: 10.1109/cvpr.2017.363. 66

[462] Y. Taigman, M. Yang, M. A. Ranzato, and L. Wolf, DeepFace: Closing the gap to human-level performance in face verification, *IEEE CVPR*, 2014. DOI: 10.1109/cvpr.2014.220. 66, 71

[463] W. Liu, Y. Wen, Z. Yu, M. Li, B. Raj, and L. Song, SphereFace: Deep hypersphere embedding for face recognition, *IEEE CVPR*, 2017. DOI: 10.1109/cvpr.2017.713. 67

[464] A. Mian, Comparison of visible, thermal infra-red and range images for face recognition, *Pacific-Rim Symposium on Image and Video Technology (PSIVT)*, Springer Lecture Notes in Computer Science (LNCS), 5414, 2009. DOI: 10.1007/978-3-540-92957-4_70. 68

[465] S. Farokhi, J. Flusser, and U. U. Sheikh, Near infrared face recognition: A literature survey, *Computer Science Review*, 21:1–17, 2016. DOI: 10.1016/j.cosrev.2016.05.003. 68, 69, 71

[466] M. Akhloufi, A. Bendada, and J.-C. Batsale, State-of-the-art in infrared face recognition, *Quantitative InfraRed Thermography Journal*, 5(1):3–26, 2008. DOI: 10.3166/qirt.5.3-26. 68, 69, 71

[467] B. Abidi, IRIS thermal/visible face database, *IEEE OTCBVS WS Series Bench*, University of Tennessee, 2005. 67

[468] S. Z. Li, R. F. Chu, S. C. Liao, and L. Zhang, Illumination invariant face recognition using near-infrared images, *IEEE Transactions on Pattern Analysis and Machine Intelligence*, 29(4):627–639, 2007. DOI: 10.1109/tpami.2007.1014. 67, 68, 70

[469] J. Bernhard, J. Barr, K. W. Bowyer, and P. Flynn, Near-IR to visible light face matching: Effectiveness of pre-processing options for commercial matchers, *IEEE International Conference on Biometrics Theory, Applications and Systems (BTAS)*, 2015. DOI: 10.1109/btas.2015.7358780. 67

[470] M. Grgic, K. Delac, and S. Grgic, SCface—surveillance cameras face database, *Multimedia Tools and Applications Journal*, 51(3):863–879, 2011. DOI: 10.1007/s11042-009-0417-2. 67

[471] B. Zhang, L. Zhang, D. Zhang, and L. Shen, Directional binary code with application to PolyU near-infrared face database, *Pattern Recognition Letters*, 31(14):2337–2344, 2010. DOI: 10.1016/j.patrec.2010.07.006. 67

[472] S. Wang, Z. Liu, Z. Wang, G. Wu, P. Shen, S. He, and X. Wang, Analyses of a multimodal spontaneous facial expression database, *IEEE Transactions on Affective Computing*, 4(1):34–46, 2013. DOI: 10.1109/t-affc.2012.32. 67

[473] A. Kumar and T. Srikanth, Online personal identification in night using multiple face representations, *ICPR*, 2008. DOI: 10.1109/icpr.2008.4761695. 67

[474] S. Z. Li, D. Yi, Z. Lei, and S. Liao, The CASIA NIR-VIS 2.0 face database, *IEEE CVPR Workshops*, 2013. DOI: 10.1109/cvprw.2013.59. 67, 72

[475] H. Steiner, S. Sporrer, A. Kolb, and N. Jung, Design of an active multispectral SWIR camera system for skin detection and face verification, *Journal of Sensors*, 2015. DOI: 10.1155/2016/9682453. 67

[476] D. A. Socolinsky and A. Selinger, A comparative analysis of face recognition performance with visible and thermal infrared imagery, *ICPR*, 2002. DOI: 10.1109/icpr.2002.1047436. 68

[477] D. Socolinsky, L. Wolff, J. Neuheisel, and C. Eveland, Illumination invariant face recognition using thermal infrared imagery, *IEEE CVPR*, 2001. DOI: 10.1109/cvpr.2001.990519. 68

[478] P. Buddharaju, I. T. Pavlidis, P. Tsiamyrtzis, and M. Bazakos, Physiology-based face recognition in the thermal infrared spectrum, *IEEE Transactions on Pattern Analysis and Machine Intelligence*, 29(4):613–626, 2007. DOI: 10.1109/tpami.2007.1007. 68

[479] R. S. Ghiass, O. Arandjelovic, A. Bendada, and X. Maldague, Vesselness features and the inverse compositional AAM for robust face recognition using thermal IR, *AAAI Conference on Artificial Intelligence*, 2013. 68, 70

[480] P. Buddharaju and I. Pavlidis, Physiological face recognition is coming of age, *IEEE CVPR*, 2009. DOI: 10.1109/cvpr.2009.5206595. 68

[481] Y. Zhou, P. Tsiamyrtzis, P. Lindner, I. Timofeyev, and I. Pavlidis, Spatiotemporal smoothing as a basis for facial tissue tracking in thermal imaging, *IEEE Transactions on Biomedical Engineering*, 60(5):1280–1289, 2013. DOI: 10.1109/tbme.2012.2232927. 68

[482] S. Taamneh et al., A multimodal dataset for various forms of distracted driving, *Scientific Data*, 4(170110), 2017. DOI: 10.1038/sdata.2017.110. 69

[483] M. J. Bihn, Evaluating short-wave infrared images on a convolutional neural network, Master's Thesis, University of Colorado, Colorado Springs, 2017. 69, 71

[484] I. Kemelmacher-Shlizerman, S. M. Seitz, D. Miller, and E. Brossard, The megaface benchmark: 1 million faces for recognition at scale, *IEEE CVPR*, 2016. DOI: 10.1109/cvpr.2016.527. 69, 71

[485] M. Turk and A. Pentland, Eigenfaces for recognition, *Journal of Cognitive Neuroscience*, 3(1):71–86, 1991. DOI: 10.1162/jocn.1991.3.1.71. 69

[486] R. Cutler, Face recognition using infrared images and eigenfaces, *Technical Report*, University of Maryland, College Park, 1996. 69

[487] C. M. Bishop, *Pattern Recognition and Machine Learning*, Springer, 2006. 69

[488] A. Selinger and D. Socolinsky, Appearance-based facial recognition using visible and thermal imagery: A comparative study, *Technical Report*, Equinox Corporation, 2002. DOI: 10.21236/ada444419. 70

[489] S. Zhao and R.-R. Grigat, An automatic face recognition system in the near infrared spectrum, *Machine Learning and Data Mining in Pattern Recognition*, Springer Lecture Notes in Computer Science (LNCS), 3587, 2005. DOI: 10.1007/11510888_43. 70

[490] J. Heo, Fusion of visual and thermal face recognition techniques: A comparative study, Master's Thesis, University of Tennessee, Knoxville, 2003. 70

[491] F. Nicolo and N. A. Schmid, A method for robust multispectral face recognition, *Image Analysis and Recognition*, Springer Lecture Notes in Computer Science (LNCS), 6754, 2011. DOI: 10.1007/978-3-642-21596-4_19. 70

[492] J. Heo, M. Savvides, and B. Vijayakumar, Performance evaluation of face recognition using visual and thermal imagery with advanced correlation filters, *IEEE International Workshop on Object Tracking and Classification Beyond the Visible Spectrum (OTCBVS)*, 2005. DOI: 10.1109/cvpr.2005.508. 70

[493] P. Buddharaju, I. Pavlidis, and I. Kakadiaris, Face recognition in the thermal infrared spectrum, *IEEE International Workshop on Object Tracking and Classification Beyond the Visible Spectrum (OTCBVS)*, 2004. DOI: 10.1109/cvpr.2004.343. 70

[494] Z. Xie, G. Liu, S. Wu, and Y. Lu, A fast infrared face recognition system using curvelet transformation, *International Symposium on Electronic Commerce and Security*, 2009. DOI: 10.1109/isecs.2009.175. 70

[495] M. Köstinger, Efficient metric learning for real-world face recognition, Dissertation, Graz University of Technology, Graz, Austria, 2013. 70

[496] P. Buddharaju, I. Pavlidis, and P. Tsiamyrtzis, Pose-invariant physiological face recognition in the thermal infrared spectrum, *IEEE CVPR Workshops*, 2006. DOI: 10.1109/cvprw.2006.160. 70

[497] Z. Xie, S. Wu, C. He, Z. Fang, and J. Yang, Infrared face recognition based on blood perfusion using bio-heat transfer model, *Chinese Conference on Pattern Recognition (CCPR)*, 2010. DOI: 10.1109/ccpr.2010.5659157. 71

[498] S. Wu, L. Wei, Z. Fang, R. Li, and X. Ye, Infrared face recognition based on blood perfusion and sub-block DCT in wavelet domain, *International Conference on Wavelet Analysis and Pattern Recognition (ICWAPR)*, 2007. DOI: 10.1109/icwapr.2007.4421626. 71

[499] M. Wang and W. Deng, Deep face recognition: A survey, *Neurocomputing*, 429:215–244, 2021. DOI: 10.1016/j.neucom.2020.10.081. 71

[500] Y. Sun, Y. Chen, X. Wang, and X. Tang, Deep learning face representation by joint identification-verification, *NIPS*, 2014. 71

[501] F. Schroff, D. Kalenichenko, and J. Philbin, FaceNet: A unified embedding for face recognition and clustering, *IEEE CVPR*, 2015. DOI: 10.1109/cvpr.2015.7298682. 71

[502] Y. Shi, X. Yu, K. Sohn, M. Chandraker, and A. K. Jain, Towards universal representation learning for deep face recognition, *IEEE CVPR*, 2020. DOI: 10.1109/cvpr42600.2020.00685. 71

[503] Y. Guo, L. Zhang, Y. Hu, X. He, and J. Gao, MS-Celeb-1M: A dataset and benchmark for large-scale face recognition, *European Conference on Computer Vision (ECCV)*, 2016. DOI: 10.1007/978-3-319-46487-9_6. 71

[504] L. Tran, X. Yin, and X. Liu, Disentangled representation learning GAN for pose-invariant face recognition, *IEEE CVPR*, 2017. DOI: 10.1109/cvpr.2017.141. 71

[505] A. T. Tran, T. Hassner, I. Masi, E. Paz, Y. Nirkin, and G. Medioni, Extreme 3D face reconstruction: Seeing through occlusions, *IEEE CVPR*, 2018. DOI: 10.1109/cvpr.2018.00414. 71

[506] J. Lezama, Q. Qiu, and G. Sapiro, Not afraid of the dark: NIR-VIS face recognition via cross-spectral hallucination and low-rank embedding, *IEEE CVPR*, 2017. DOI: 10.1109/cvpr.2017.720. 71

[507] X. Y. Jing, F. Wu, X. Zhu, X. Dong, F. Ma, and Z. Li, Multi-spectral low-rank structured dictionary learning for face recognition, *Pattern Recognition*, 59:14–25, 2016. DOI: 10.1016/j.patcog.2016.01.023. 71

[508] R. Raghavendra, B. Dorizzi, A. Rao, and G. H. Kumar, Particle swarm optimization based fusion of near infrared and visible images for improved face verification, *Pattern Recognition*, 44(2):401–411, 2011. DOI: 10.1016/j.patcog.2010.08.006. 71

[509] F. Omri, S. Foufou, and M. Abidi, NIR and visible image fusion for improving face recognition at long distance, *International Conference on Image and Signal Processing*, Springer Lecture Notes in Computer Science (LNCS), 8509, 2014. DOI: 10.1007/978-3-319-07998-1_63. 71

[510] F. Wu, X. Jing, X. Dong, R. Hu, D. Yue, L. Wang, Y. Ji, R. Wang, and G. Chen, Intraspectrum discrimination and interspectrum correlation analysis deep network for multi-spectral face recognition, *IEEE Transactions on Cybernetics*, 50(3):1009–1022, 2020. DOI: 10.1109/tcyb.2018.2876591. 71

[511] G. Bebis, A. Gyaourova, S. Singh, and I. Pavlidis, Face recognition by fusing thermal infrared and visible imagery, *Image and Vision Computing*, 24(7):727–742, 2006. DOI: 10.1016/j.imavis.2006.01.017. 71

[512] S. G. Kong, J. Heo, F. Boughorbel, Y. Zheng, B. R. Abidi, A. Koschan, M. Yi, and M. A. Abidi, Multiscale fusion of visible and thermal IR images for illumination-invariant face recognition, *International Journal of Computer Vision (IJCV)*, 71(2):215–233, 2007. DOI: 10.1007/s11263-006-6655-0. 71

[513] E. Kaziakhmedov, K. Kireev, G. Melnikov, M. Pautov, and A. Petiushko, Real-world attack on MTCNN face detection system, *IEEE International Multi-Conference on Engineering, Computer and Information Sciences*, 2019. DOI: 10.1109/sibircon48586.2019.8958122. 72

[514] S. Iranmanesh, B. Riggan, S. Hu, and N. Nasrabadi, Coupled generative adversarial network for heterogeneous face recognition, *Image and Vision Computing (IVC)*, 94, 2020. DOI: 10.1016/j.imavis.2019.103861. 72, 73

[515] C. Fondje, S. Hu, N. Short, and B. Riggan, Cross-domain identification for thermal-to-visible face recognition, *IEEE International Joint Conference on Biometrics (IJCB)*, 2020. DOI: 10.1109/ijcb48548.2020.9304937. 72, 73

[516] B. Riggan, S. Reale, and N. Nasrabadi, Coupled auto-associative neural networks for heterogeneous face recognition, *IEEE Access*, 3, 2015. DOI: 10.1109/access.2015.2479620. 72

[517] M. Rezaei and R. Klette, *Computer Vision for Driver Assistance—Simultaneous Traffic and Driver Monitoring*, Springer, 2017. DOI: 10.1007/978-3-319-50551-0. 73

[518] J. Janai, F. Güney, A. Behl, and A. Geiger, Computer vision for autonomous vehicles: Problems, datasets and state-of-the-art, *ArXiv:1704.05519*, 2021. 73

[519] P. Liu, M. Geppert, L. Heng, T. Sattler, A. Geiger, and M. Pollefeys, Towards robust visual odometry with a multi-camera system, *IEEE/RSJ International Conference on Intelligent Robots and Systems (IROS)*, 2018. DOI: 10.1109/iros.2018.8593561. 73

[520] V. Kachurka, D. Roussel, H. Hadj-Abdelkader, F. Bonardi, J.-Y. Didier, and S. Bouchafa, SWIR camera-based localization and mapping in challenging environments, *International Conference on Image Analysis and Processing (ICIAP)*, 2019. DOI: 10.1007/978-3-030-30645-8_41. 74

[521] M. Kim, S. Joung, K. Park, S. Kim, and K. Sohn, Unpaired cross-spectral pedestrian detection via adversarial feature learning, *IEEE ICIP*, 2019. DOI: 10.1109/icip.2019.8803098. 75

[522] P. Addabbo, A. Angrisano, M. Bernardi, G. Gagliarde, A. Mennella, M. Nisi, and S. Ullo, A UAV infrared measurement approach for defect detection in photovoltaic plants, *IEEE International Workshop on Metrology for AeroSpace (MetroAeroSpace)*, 2017. DOI: 10.1109/metroaerospace.2017.7999594. 75

[523] C. Burke, P. R. McWhirter, J. Veitch-Michaelis, O. McAree, H. Pointon, S. Wich, and S. Longmore, Requirements and limitations of thermal drones for effective search and rescue in marine and coastal areas, *Drones*, 3(4), 2019. DOI: 10.3390/drones3040078. 75

[524] C. Yuan, Z. Liu, and Y. Zhang, Fire detection using infrared images for UAV-based forest fire surveillance, *International Conference on Unmanned Aircraft Systems*, 2017. DOI: 10.1109/icuas.2017.7991306. 75

[525] A. Shamsoshoara, F. Afghah, A. Razi, L. Zheng, P. Z. Fule, and E. Blasch, Aerial imagery pile burn detection using deep learning: The FLAME dataset, *Computer Networks*, 193, 2021. DOI: 10.1016/j.comnet.2021.108001. 75

[526] W. Frodella, M. Elashvili, D. Spizzichino, G. Gigli, L. Adikashvili, N. Vacheishvili, G. Kirkitadze, A. Nadaraia, C. Margottini, and N. Casagli, Combining infrared thermography and UAV digital photogrammetry for the protection and conservation of rupestrian cultural heritage sites in Georgia: A methodological application, *Remote Sensing*, 12:2–25, 2020. DOI: 10.3390/rs12050892. 75

[527] R. Zhang, H. Li, K. Duan, S. You, K. Liu, F. Wang, and Y. Hu, Automatic detection of earthquake-damaged buildings by integrating UAV oblique photography and infrared thermal imaging, *Remote Sensing*, 12:2–27, 2020. DOI: 10.3390/rs12162621. 75

[528] D. Andritoiu, L. Bazavan, F. Besnea, H. Roibu, and N. Bizdoaca, Agriculture autonomous monitoring and decisional mechatronic system, *19th International Carpathian Control Conference*, 2018. DOI: 10.1109/carpathiancc.2018.8399635. 75

[529] P. Lottes, R. Khanna, J. Pfeifer, R. Siegwart, and C. Stachniss, UAV-based crop and weed classification for smart farming, *IEEE International Conference on Robotics and Automation (ICRA)*, 2017. DOI: 10.1109/icra.2017.7989347. 74, 75

[530] R Argolo dos Santos, E. Chartuni Mantovani, R. Filgueiras, E. Inácio Fernandes-Filho, A. Cristielle Barbosa da Silva, and L. Peroni Venancio, Actual evapotranspiration and biomass of maize from a red-green-near-infrared (RGNIR) sensor on board an unmanned aerial vehicle (UAV), *Water*, 12:2–20, 2020. DOI: 10.3390/w12092359. 75

[531] A. Jenal, G. Bareth, A. Bolten, C. Kneer, I. Weber, and J. Bongartz, Development of a VNIR/SWIR multispectral imaging system for vegetation monitoring with unmanned aerial vehicles, *Sensors*, 19(24), 2019. DOI: 10.3390/s19245507. 75

[532] V. Saiz-Rubio and F. Rovira-Más, From smart farming towards agriculture 5.0: A review on crop data management, *Agronomy*, 10:2–21, 2020. DOI: 10.3390/agronomy10020207. 74, 75

[533] K. C. Santosh, S. Antani, D. S. Guru, and N. Dey, *Medical Imaging—Artificial Intelligence, Image Recognition, and Machine Learning Techniques*, CRC Press, 2019. DOI: 10.1201/9780429029417. 79

[534] S. K. Zhou, D. Rueckert, and G. Fichtinger, *Handbook of Medical Image Computing and Computer Assisted Intervention*, Academic Press, 2019. DOI: 10.1016/c2017-0-04608-6. 79

# Authors' Biographies

## MICHAEL TEUTSCH

**Michael Teutsch** received his diploma degree in computer science and his Ph.D. degree from the Karlsruhe Institute of Technology (KIT) in 2009 and 2014, respectively. From 2009–2016 he worked as a research scientist and a postdoc at the Fraunhofer IOSB, Karlsruhe, Germany. Since 2016, he has been with Hensoldt Optronics, Oberkochen, Germany. His research interests include computer vision, visual surveillance, object detection, object tracking, and machine learning. Michael has been organizing and co-chairing the annual IEEE International Workshop on Perception Beyond the Visible Spectrum (PBVS) in conjunction with the IEEE International Conference on Computer Vision and Pattern Recognition (CVPR) since 2018. He is active as lecturer in computer vision currently at the Baden-Wuerttemberg Cooperative State University (DHBW) Heidenheim, Germany. Michael serves as reviewer for several journals and conferences such as *IEEE Transactions on Pattern Analysis and Machine Intelligence* (TPAMI), *IEEE Transactions on Circuits and Systems for Video Technology* (TCSVT), or *IEEE Transactions on Geoscience and Remote Sensing* (TGRS). He has authored or co-authored more than 30 scientific publications.

## ANGEL D. SAPPA

**Angel D. Sappa** received his Electro Mechanical Engineering degree (1995) from National University of La Pampa, Argentina, and his Ph.D. degree in Industrial Engineering (1999) from Polytechnic University of Catalonia, Barcelona, Spain. In 2003, after research positions in France (LAAS-CNRS), the UK (UK Advanced Robotics), and Greece (ITI-CERTH), he joined the Computer Vision Center, Barcelona, Spain, where he currently holds a Senior Scientist position. Since 2016 he has been a full professor at the ESPOL Polytechnic University, Guayaquil, Ecuador, where he leads the computer vision team at CIDIS research center; he is the director of the Electrical Engineering Ph.D. program. His research interests include cross-spectral image processing and representation; 3D data acquisition, processing, and modeling; and computer vision applications. He published about 200 papers in international journals and conference proceedings and served as program committee member in several international conferences. He has been involved in several national, regional, and international research projects and several technological transfer projects; he has been the cofounder of VINTRA Inc. (San Francisco, USA) and Crowdmobile S.L. (Barcelona, Spain). He is a Senior Member of the Institute of Electrical and Electronics Engineers (IEEE).

## RIAD I. HAMMOUD

**Riad I. Hammoud** received an M.S. degree in Controls of Systems and a Ph.D. in Computer Vision and Robotics from UTC and INRIA (France) late 1997 and early 2001, respectively. He did his postdoc at Indiana University in 2002. Since early 2003, he has been working on several projects involving infrared imaging for defense, automotive, and robotics applications. Early 2019, he joined TuSimple to develop autonomous driving systems. From 2012–2019, he worked at BAE Systems (Boston, MA, USA), on DARPA, AFRL, and other U.S. government agencies' advanced research projects as principal investigator (PI), team lead, and research scientist. Before joining BAE Systems, Riad was at Tobii-Dynavox (Pittsburgh, PA, USA) and Delphi Automotive Systems (Kokomo, IN, USA) working on Assistive Technologies and Active Safety Systems. He joined Seth Teller's team at MIT as a collaborating Researcher to work on the DARPA Robotics Challenge (2012–2015). Dr. Riad Hammoud served as guest editor of several special issues of top journals in computer vision including *CVIU* and *IJCV*. He authored several edited book including the Springer book on *Augmented Vision Perception in Infrared*. Since 2004, he has been organizing and chairing a workshop series in conjunction with the IEEE CVPR on Perception Beyond the Visible Spectrum (PBVS). He also serves as the general chair of SPIE Automatic Target Recognition conference (2018–2021).

Printed in the United States
by Baker & Taylor Publisher Services